The Devil's Diary XIII

Walpurgisnacht XLIII Anno Satanas

Front Cover Art : Anton LaVey Tribute by Draconis Blackthorne.
Back Cover Art: Magus LaVey Tribute Gallery by Draconis Blackthorne.

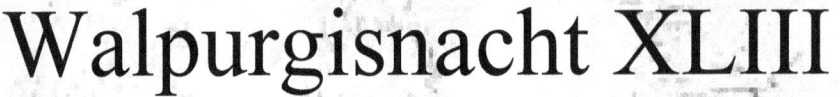

Walpurgisnacht XLIII

On this traditional Witch's Sabbath, do we recognize the foundation of The Church of Satan on that historic night within black candle-lit halls, reverberating darkened reflections from timeless celebrations afore, and from the Trapezohedron Gates of Hell were unleashed the Daemons of realization and creation.

Since that inception has The Infernal Empire continually thrived and grown, igniting the black flame upon the crowns of carnal devils across The Earth, who in turn wield our passions, further strengthening this tenebrous Cabal. Indeed, from the darkness of The Abyss within do come many wondrous things... and so it shall ever be.

Shemhamforash! Hail The Church of Satan!

In Nomine Satanas,

Warlock Draconis Blackthorne
Walpurgisnacht, XLIII A.S.
Noctuary, The Infernal Empire

New Year XLIII A.S.

Greetings Satanists!

A toast! I lift a glass of Leviathan's finest philtres to us all! To another indulgent year of Creativity and Strength!

Sign the Pact for resolutions for the coming year to manifest The Will... all that has been proposed this past year has been fulfilled, as we move forward in continued success!

The treasures of The Black Earth belong to us! Partake in the bounty of The Devil's Cornucopia, in all of their myriad carnal delights!

Here's to Year XLIII! Shemhamforash! Hail SATAN!

SO IT IS DONE.

In Nomine Satanas,
Warlock Draconis Blackthorne
January 1, XLIII A.S.
Noctuary, The Infernal Empire

Vernal Equinox XLIII A.S.

T he seasons are in flux as new life comes forth, to be devoured by snarling beasts or propagated in darkened lairs, as libertine satyrs, incubi, and lush nymphs, succubi, dance the dance of life in gardens of indulgence and opulent pantheons of fleshly delights.

Intoxicating aromas pervade the senses, as storms whirl in transformation and rejuvenation, impregnating the black earth with streams of vital nectar, laden into caverns of blossoming effervescence. The bounty of the land overflows with succulent ambrosia, as carnal gods and goddesses partake in deepest epicurean pleasure.

The Scarlet Woman rides the Beast, prepare the voluptuously lascivious feast!

Strength through Joy! Regie Satanas! Ave Satanas! Hail Lilith! Hail Satan!

SO IT IS DONE.

In Nomine Satanas,

Warlock Draconis Blackthorne
Church of Satan Warlock
The Haunted Noctuary, Infernal Empire

Life Is The Great Indulgence!
Paul Hill

Being a human animal I know that I am responsible for my life and that no fictional god or angel is going to give me anything, so I always knew that if I was going to enjoy the only life I have it was going to all be on my shoulders as to how it turns out. And being realistic and never wanting to be a psychic vampire I knew that in order to enjoy my only life I was also going to have to be responsible for it as well. So I went to college while I was working full-time to support myself knowing that it was the only way to survive. After all, self-preservation is the highest law. I also knew that somewhere down the road I would have to reward myself for my hard work and very high grades knowing that there are so many things in this world to enjoy, so I tried to incorporate whenever I could between my responsibility's any kind of enjoyment possible.

Aside from being an Accounting and Administrator Associate in various different roles over the years in the corporate world to support myself, I also started doing both college and professional radio that was in front of and behind the microphone as these were some of things I had always wanted to experience. And getting to meet some of the radio personalities that I grew up with as well, along with a couple of other celebrities. I even had the joy of co-hosting a college radio show with a buddy of mine for a few years, playing the music that we liked and talking about what we wanted to talk about. Also during the last several years I have had the pleasure of writing dozens of articles and some reviews for some of the best Satanic publications around which is something that I have very much enjoyed. And best of all I have had the pleasure of travelling all over the Caribbean on Royal Caribbean cruise lines and having a wonderful time on many of the different tropical islands down there. It was great getting to meet not only different people from all over America, but from other countries around the world as well. It was especially interesting to try and experiment with all of the different drinks that I learned about from them on top of all the wonderful array of tropical drinks that I was already enjoying there!

I loved getting to experience and enjoy the atmosphere as well as the various music of Reggae and Jimmy Buffet and Hawaiian tunes, etc. It is such a contrast compared to where I live in Chicago. Being from Chicago which is a world class city with everything from the worlds best shopping and museums to the Theater, Jewelry, and Financial Districts. As well as having so many of the worlds tallest buildings around, plus there are dozens of subways, elevated trains and different types of Metra trains everywhere. Yes, I love trains. Chicago is somewhat similar to the islands in one way though with the miles of beautiful beaches that have impressed even people from California and Florida. Then you go from the big city to the tropical world of palm trees and endless ocean waters and always wondering about all of the incredible sea life that lives in the great waters of Leviathan. So that is when I decided to try some things like going on island tours that included going in the water with dolphins and riding on mini submarines to explore beneath the ocean, as well as snorkeling with an underwater camera to take close up photos of the amazing different life forms that live in the tropical waters.

Among other things that I love doing is studying all of the different religion's that man kind has created over these centuries. As well as reading about different philosophy's and occult practices and experimenting with them. After all as a Satanist I am not afraid of exploring the Unknown, the Dark Side or the Hidden and do not see it as evil like so many limiting religion's do since you are suppose to put your whole life in the hands of some insane man made god. Happily I am part of a religion that doesn't hamper your knowledge or enjoyment of life with silly restrictions that are so unnatural.

I also love my music whether it is various different types of Heavy Metal, Alternative Rock or some of the many different types of tropical music. I have even had the pleasure of chatting with some of my favorite musicians such as King Diamond, Vincent Crowley of Acheron and Thomas Thorn of the Electric Hellfire Club. I have also enjoyed many great movies over the years. Especially some of the good monster and horror movies like the classics from Universal studios as well as Britain's Hammer and others with their famous monsters and the actors that portray them, about as much as I enjoy some of the modern day horror films. Of course as we all know the theater like everything in life was once forbidden by the Christians as they saw the theater as the "Devils Lantern" and a way to summon Satan into your life. Just like they once considered all music and dancing a one way ticket to hell because any and all entertainment is all a part of the Devils work.

How wonderful it is to enjoy the only life we will ever have instead of wasting it on fearing death or worshipping some non-existent god that even if it did exist doesn't give a damn about anyone or anything. So use that time and energy to do the things you enjoy and explore the world we live in because you only have this one opportunity to do so. Live and enjoy, feed the demon within yourself with pleasure. After all the watchword of Satanism is "Indulgence".

"Heads Up" With Reverend Chris Redstar

An interview by Tier Instinct

A massive resurgence in the sport of poker has taken place over the last decade, and shows no signs of slowing down anytime soon. The game is played at home, in casinos, and tournaments now world wide. Broadcasting of the sport has become a high demand among it's viewers, and has given celebrity status to many professional players. The most popular form of poker is Texas Hold'em.

Players from all walks of life now flock to casinos, online gaming tables, and tournaments for a chance at riches and a shot at knocking out a pro. Tournaments like the World Series of Poker, and the World Poker Tour, now draw participants way into the thousands. Each year poker draws more players than the last, but standing in their way is CoS Reverend, Chris Redstar.

Reverend Chris Redstar is a member of the Priesthood of Mendes, and media spokesperson for the Church of Satan in Germany. He is an author, artist, and professional poker player. In this interview, Rev. Redstar offers up his perspective on the game of poker, and just what it takes to survive at the tables. A rare treat for Satanists who enjoy the game of poker, and a nice read for anyone who is interested in the game.

The Devils Diary: *What attracts you to the game of Poker?*

Reverend Chris Redstar: Poker is a mirror of life. People compete for money, honor, and respect. Every mistake, every bad decision will be punished right on the spot. Every good decision will be rewarded. Pure stratification at work .I am a very competitive person. I love the mind wars at the table. I want to destroy my opponents mentally and then finish them off by taking all their money. When you sit at the table, it's not the cards you hold that matters. It's what your opponent thinks about your cards. Poker is your every-day's life in a nutshell.

TDD: *When do you know to continue playing, or to quit?*

CR: Compare it with a relationship. How often have you thought: "Hey, I should leave now. It makes no sense anymore." And how often did you stay to give it another chance? Did it ever work out well? I doubt it. Trust your feeling. When you feel your judgments at the table go worse, then leave. When everything goes your way and luck slaps you in the face, then stay and enjoy as long as it lasts. And like in a relationship, every partner is different and makes you a different couple with different habits, every table is different in the same way. No game is like the one before.

TDD: *What has been your biggest moment in Poker?*

CR: Money wise, it was a $30.000 pot I won in online poker at the $200/$400 No Limit Hold'em table. I won $42.000 that night and at that time, this meant the world to me. I lost so much money outside of gambling in that year, due to private problems. Emotionally my biggest moment was playing against Gus Hansen and Mike Matusow at the same table in a Pot Limit Omaha game on Full Tilt Poker.

TDD: *When you are not playing poker, what are some other games you play to stay sharp?*

CR: When I am not playing Poker, I work for a major online Poker company, try to finish my new book and work on many different art projects with my wife, CoS Witch Melanie Laetitia Mantis [laetitiasdeath.com]. So you can see, there is not much time left for other games. I do play some slots, when I am in Vegas, but that's pretty much it. I would love to play more games of skill. Maybe I will have more time in a few years.

TDD: *What aspect of Satanism do you see in the game of poker?*

CR: - Stratification. Very clearly. Only a few survive in Poker. Most players go broke time and time again. - Survival of the fittest. Only people with passion and self-control at the same time can prevail in such emotional battles. - The need to learn from mistakes. A basic Satanic virtue - the need to combine all your abilities to win. Nobody is perfect, but life just like Poker forces you to use your strength and to exercise your weaker aspects. Intelligence alone gets you nowhere.

Combine experience, instinct and intelligence and you have a Satanist, or a poker player (which is not necessarily the same).

TDD: *Do you feel being a Satanist, gives you an advantage at the tables?*

CR: Not in general. But certain aspects of a Satanic personality are definitely good at the tables. Analytical thinking, i.e., being a good judge of character is not bad either. I think anybody who is able to swing between the two extremes of canceling all emotions and creating a ritual environment at the table is a good player. You need to be extreme at the table in every possible way, if that makes any sense to you.

TDD: *When did you first play Poker?*

CR: I started to play 5-card draw when I was 10. We were playing for pennies or marbles if we had nothing else. My first experience with Hold 'em was when I was 16 and I play in casinos since the age of 21. Limit Hold 'em and Stud were the only games they offered until the Moneymaker effect set in.

TDD: *What prompted you to play Professional?*

CR: I decided to play poker professionally (as a season pro) because there is so much money in that game. Compared to 10 years ago, you have 90% donkeys now. A lot of players see poker as a game of chance, even if they don't admit it, they play like it. They are giving their money away and

I like to take advantage of that. This year, I mainly play the $25/$50 limit games and $10/$20 no limit Hold'em and Pot Limit Omaha. I can make more money in a week than in any other job in 6 months.

TDD: *Who is you biggest rival in Poker, and why?*

CR: There is not a certain person whom I might call a rival, because I rarely play in the same places. My typical rival is a maniac show off, who thinks poker is a cock comparison competition. The "I raise you whatever you have" type of guy can be fair game, but every now and then he costs you a fortune and will tell you all night long how good he plays. Take the game of Gus Hanson and the mouth of Mike Matusow, and you know what I mean.

———

Much appreciation to Reverend Redstar for participating in this interview for **The Devil's Diary**.

The Time Travel Chamber
Ritual of Evocation, A Remembrance & Actualization of Past Orthodoxies
Draconis Blackthorne

~ Introduction ~

Purpose & Definition

This asserts the principle of The Timeless All-One of The Self, as we exist in a transformative reality, which will furthermore access dormant memory cells to actualize into the eternal now. Mind controls matter, and here you are exercising the principle of becoming yourself as you wish to be, as the potential is already within. Past, Present, and Future are concurrent, so it is up to you wherein you wish to reside.

Endeavor to replicate with as much detail possible, environments of your formative development, Now that technology has progressed to such a point where our evocations can be much more suitably collected and arranged to approximation, gather all elements which you may have in your possession, or which may be obtained through various sources, and begin arranging rooms {or one's Ritual Chamber, or even sections of a room, somewhat resembling shrines of Oneself} where one may completely immerse oneself in that reality.

Descriptions

Image of Oneself in particular phase centered upon a table or pedestal, surrounded with accoutrements of specification. May also expand to encompass an entire room.

* Formative development: *Pre-pubescence.*

Anywhere from infancy through to about 9-12 cycles. May include cradle, favored toys, clothing, photos, familiar images, posters, decor, colorations, to various other items such as music, literature, films, even food, and certain scents.

* The Awakening: *Pubescence.* {"teenage" development}.

From 13-18-21 cycles. The "party room" as it were. May include clothing, photos, familiar images, posters, decor, colorations, to various other items such as music, literature, films, even food, and certain scents.

* *Future Room.*

Here you are creating a reality that shall materialize in actual form and in grander scale. Arrangements include clothing, photos, familiar images, posters, decor, colorations, to various other items such as music, even food, and certain scents, all as you wish them to be as identical as possible, from photographs, sculptures, to drawn images, the purpose is to meditate upon their materialization, creating a sympathetic dynamic.

Process

Go forth into your Time Travel Chamber, taking care to not be disturbed, meditating upon the atmosphere for a while, acclimating and visualizing oneself in that state of physical formation. Bring to mind pleasant memories, re-experiencing them as they surface, and acting accordingly.

If there is a monitor in the room, play a favored presentation in appropriation to the room of purpose; and/or play music accordingly, and/or read literature from that frame. If possible, these appliances should be models from that period, otherwise these should remain hidden.

Optional: One may begin and end within The Ritual Chamber, enunciating the preliminary instructions of ritual from *The Satanic Bible*.

[This is an addendum to the "Timeless Machine" in *Dracomeroth.*]

Additional reading: "Evocation", "A Medicine For Melancholy", "Erotic Crystallization Inertia", The Devil's Notebook. "Time Travel, Cheap & Easy", The Satanic Scriptures.

Observations Inside & Outside The Ritual Chamber
by Jan Welke

For quite a while now, I have observed an interesting phenomenon inside of the ritual chamber and the rooms in close proximity to it that I would like to share.

On several occasions, there have been unusual occurrences in the room that I use as my ritual chamber, mainly after a ritual has been performed or shortly before. They mainly consist in disturbances concerning the electricity supply and irregularities in the way electric and electronic devices work when run in the chamber. Of course, these might also partly result from a slightly defective electricity supply, but they also occur on notebooks which are used without plug. Programs do not work properly and the system breaks down more frequently. In addition, technical devices run by batteries do react in a similar way.

Light bulbs quit their service more frequently, which has led me to purchase larger quantities of them just in case. What appears to be even more peculiar is that the light bulbs are slightly flickering from time to time even though the bulbs as such are intact. Then I have this big lamp which utters a clicking noise every now and then, especially when switched on after a ritual has been performed.

A further observation is that CD played on my stereo which I have placed in the respective room behave oddly as well, in so far that the music played is sometimes accompanied by scratching sounds or the CD player jumps to a different track, even though the given CD looks perfectly intact.

It has to be noted that such phenomena take place anywhere that I have practiced rituals over a period of time. While in Romania, I first tended to sometimes explain it away to be a consequence of the Romanian electricity supply not being as reliable as the one in Germany. In so far, disturbances were to be expected to some degree. This is nothing unusual during a fall-out. However, the irregularities took place regardless whether there had been a fall-out shortly before or after or not. Regardless of the place, the similarities are truly stunning.

Apart from that, the fact that the other rooms of the apartment do not turn out to be as striking in this regard, makes me assume that there is a different cause.

Additionally, said rituals appear to coincide with certain incidents only indirectly related to myself and my lair. However, these side effects are fairly welcome, even if they are not been precisely made mention of as a desired outcome. Of course, I do fully approve of the annoying drunkard three houses down the road having a heart attack, especially as I do well recall him dropping his bottles in front of my house in the middle of the night as well as shouting loudly out of his mind. Anything that serves to purge the area around me from such type of wastrels is perfectly fine. May the shockwave blow them away from my map!

All in all, I have come to consider the named occurrences signs proving that magical workings performed in the ritual chamber have released a certain amount of energy which also effects the immediate surrounding, so to say as a side-effect. Something is so-to-say in the works.

And at the same time, I thank this magnificent side-effect the spooky note that it adds to my lair. It serves well to scare off any sort of intruder. The described oddities fit in perfectly with my obsession for old and antique furniture, books, weapons and rare items of all kind to provide this lair with the appeal of a haunted place, in which has stopped a hundred years ago.

Furthermore, it makes this place even more extraordinary as it harbours a chamber that presents a gateway to manifest my impact on the world outside of that haunted little room.

It is this world outside of the intellectual decompression chamber, the structure of which magic aims to alter. The confident magician who has been freed from his emotional baggage re-enters this structure again and may at first experience what one might call a stagnating phase, in which no proof of his working's impact is to be found. Yet, as the irregularities I have witnessed in my lair prove, the energies have been sent and transmission is already taking place.

What might at first glance look like state of stagnation, turns out to be something entirely different under the surface oftentimes. Behind the curtain the scene is already being re-arranged. Sometimes, its structure is affected in absolutely unexpected ways. It could be that issues and projects that have already gathered dust are all of a sudden infused with a vital dynamic again to bring forth marvellous fruits. As unlikely as it may appear, chain reactions are initiated from time to time which make their way towards the desired result. In so far, what one notices as odd occurrences in one's ritual chamber at first could already present the first element of this miraculous chain of events.

Mmmmmmm... Meat.... Or Why Carnivorous Satanists are A-OK.

Lady Blackthorne

Like it or not, we humans basically top the food chain. For the most part, we are tirsiary consumers, meaning that we eat the animals that eat the animals, who eat the plants. The Tenth Rule of The Earth states that the only reason to harm animals is for self-defense or for food. Predatory behavior is all natural. LaVey knew it {any natural Satanist should know it instinctually}, and he made no bones about it.

Philosophically, Satanists should have no problem eating other animals. By and large, Satanists will realize that even though an animal died to yield the slab on their plate, the animal was raised to be meat, thus the animals' highest purpose will be fulfilled. If the Satanist in question prefers to kill their own meat {a-la Ted Nugent}, chances are the Satanist will realize the sacrifice made by the animal to sustain his/her own life, and will savor every bite, appreciating the nutrients fully provided by the ex-fellow living creature. In any case, the Satanist will have observed and upheld the highest law - self-preservation.

If for some reason I myself cannot comprehend, the Satanist chooses to be a vegetarian, he/she will most likely have the common sense to realize a few things your average PETA-worshipper will not. For one, their "veggieism" is a choice, and should not be forced upon others who do not share his/her views. Also as a human, they are free to make this choice for themselves, but they will recognize that their pets {if any} have different, more specific nutritional needs, and will still provide a commercial pet food for them, even if it contains miscellaneous animal parts. Finally, if the nutritional needs of the Satanist should change {i.e., through pregnancy, disease, or physical training}, he/she will realize that soy beans and tofu soup will no longer cut it, and they must return to eating meat to maintain their overall health. If not, deterioration will be imminent.

But don't take my word for it.

I encourage you, dear reader, to look at the average herbivorous human. For the most part, they are thin, almost sickly. After too long, the body deprived of meat protein will begin to become weak, bones brittle, muscles under-developed. Males will become impotent and females unable to bear children. Arthritis will ensue. Unless one is extremely careful, over the years, the herbivorous human will slowly starve themselves to death. Why? Because we are *omnivores*. We need our veggies as much as we need our meat. If one walks away from a study of Satanism with only one thing, it should be this: balance in the individual as in nature, is key to vital existence. This having been said, to place yourself firmly at one extreme or the other will most likely be a threat to one's existence. To purposefully put yourself out of balance runs counter to the idea of self-preservation, being the highest law in nature. Yes, you CAN be a Satanist AND a meat-eater, as long as you eat your veggies too.

N64 TOTAL ENVIRONMENTS
by Jan Welke

Although current consoles have perfected animations, graphics and sound, Nintendo's N64 still remains my favourite of all. The 3D animation made it outstanding at that time and can still provide for a splendid playing experience nowadays, especially for a brief session every now and then. Moreover, its slight out-datedness compared to today's standards and imperfection in regard to graphics and animation lend it a unique character that occasionally reminds of arcade video-games 10 or 15 years ago. Very much like its precedent the SNES, many of the games combine a good storyline with a thrilling atmosphere, flair, lots of special features, charismatic characters plus most games offered on this system are not too complicated in terms of controls. Unlike most video game systems, this one corresponds in a magnificent way with my aesthetic preferences.

vAmong others, I still prefer playing the following N64 game classics:

Castlevania which is a mixture of adventure, jump'n run and action game certainly still has its place among my favourites.

The plot being Transylvania in the 19th century, the environment consists of haunted castles, gloomy deserted landscapes and forests and the likes. This results in a dark and bewitched atmosphere to immediately consume those who appreciate this type of aesthetics. Within these surroundings, the player has to fight against monsters, vampires, ghosts and other creature emerging from the dark side in order to find hidden items and secret doorways and battle his way towards Count Dracula's castle to finally confront him. The player will face a series of shocking surprise attacks, thrilling battles and demanding tasks to fulfil.

Belonging to the later generation of games at that time, *007 - The World Is Not Enough* is one of the outstanding games available on that system and still my favourite ego-shooter.

It is in fact closely related to the game Golden Eye which unfortunately had been banned in a few countries of Europe due to violent contents. The little rumble pack adds the splendid sensation of being a real part of the virtual reality explored. The numerous weapons that are waiting to be acquired turn the game into a true delight for everyone into firearms. One of the superb traits consists in the variety of multiplayer modes and options which the game offers. Of course, everyone who enjoys the technical gadgets and devices that make the James Bond movies so unique will be delighted concerning the equipment that awaits the player.

A similarly entertaining ego-shooter to be explored is certainly *Perfect Dark*. In regard to the variety of weapons, gadgets and special equipment to be collected and applied it is similar to 007, however here it is more of a Science Fiction storyline and plot, being that the protagonist, the stunning Joanne Dark, attempts to stop a conspiracy carried out by extraterrestrial opponents. She fights her way through the many levels that provide perfect environments to explore. Among other exciting tasks, freeing hostages, precise assassinations and deactivating explosives are part of the mission. Furthermore, the combat simulator is available which in fact is a game in itself, offering a wide range of options for single- and multiplayer modes. Many more demanding missions are to be carried out here.

All in all, the mentioned video-games make for ideal total environments, conveying a dense and thrilling atmosphere which the player is drawn into step by step. Due to the technical possibilities of that time, the animations have mainly been reduced to the basics and yet still realistic enough for the player to identify with the character. Besides, in my personal opinion, a video game does not have to be completely robbed of the characteristics of artificiality to make for exciting entertainment.

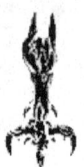

Noctuarium

QuickTime™ and a
GIF decompressor
are needed to see this picture.

Multimedia Reviews

{Reviews by Draconis Blackthorne unless otherwise noted.}

Satan's Scroll
Bibliography Reviews

Not Like Most 17
XLIII - XLIV. Purging Talon Publishing

Not Like Most 17In this edition, On The Infernal Front contains the latest evilutions occurring within The Infernal Empire, from the superb bibliography unleashed within "The Year of Satanic Literature", The Satanic Calendar, to several musical manifestations, including The Black House: A Tribute to Anton S. LaVey, the pleasing continuance of Radio Free Satan, and the stimulating resurgence of Satanism Today.

Also introducing the issue is a touching eulogy for Warlock Crowclaws by Bill M., describing Shawn's irrefutable impact on the 'Witch City', the realization of himself as a Satanist, which proved to be a veritable zeitgeist in its transformation.

A favored piece herein is Reverend Moore's haunting tales of his experiences living in Horrorweird land {and the San Fernando Valley in Los Diablos, which this reviewer can relate to}, the many interesting synchronicities associated with Ed Wood, and his and Priestess Sinnz's compelling friendship with legendary screen maven Maila "Vampira" Nurmi.

Magister Sprague posits critical analysis on pretentious internet behavior in The Awkward Road To Satanism. Intellectual Black Holes abound! It bears restating to the sincerely interested, that before engaging in educated conversations about Satanism, the pre-requisite is to read and study The Satanic Bible first.

Next we are treated to Satanism and Atheism, from Magister Svengali. Indeed, Satanism begins with Atheism. Following is another treat - this one from Magister Paradise's book Bearing The Devil's Mark, with an excerpt from the chapter entitled "Further Evidence of The Satanic Age", both of which I heartily agree with.

The Mediabolica section features many reviews by several authors on a variety of multimedia sources, inclusive of Year XLII's splendid literary proliferation. Magister Paradise also graciously reviews The Devil's Diary Issues 9-12, among other remarkable publications.

Also of note, the inclusion of a great interview conducted by Tekku with Warlocks Menta and Asec Zonei, discussing all the intriguing elements which went into the creation of The Black House: A Tribute to Anton S. LaVey CD, followed by a personal relation of Colonel Akula's activities in the great outdoors. Salaciously metaphorical fiction jolts the senses in "Big Bertha's Mystic Striptease", while Magister Paulis realistically dissects the societal notion that one's career also be a pleasure, which apparently seems to be less often than so {if it is, that is wonderful, and why not strive to make it so? Knowing oneself honestly and pursuing one's passions are the key to materializing that pleasant situation; however, the herd are often deluded into considering it so when it is not, and thus, remain enslaved, where they belong}. Also included is an amusing parody ad for "Stay Brite" toothpaste by Rev. Mealie, featuring an array of distinctive dental patients. {"Breath... Taste... Teeth...!"}

Highly recommended, Not Like Most remains a most entertaining and pleasing publication, inspiring mental gratification and carnal contemplation. Two Horns Up!

The Ninth Gate
{#3 Halloween XLII A.S.}

The Ninth GateThis issue is a veritable tribute to Vlad Tepes, containing all things about The Impaler and the Vampiric genre, from artistry {the portrait of Vlad and the historical observation on the Voivod's artistic representations by Warlock Nocturnum}, to statuary, jewelry, photography, poetry, music, intriguing film reviews, salacious gothic fetish models, to hypothetical statements, several interviews with proprietors {Nightshade, Vampire Wear}, authors {Michelle Belanger},

musicians {Anders Manga, Theatres Des Vampires, Soulfyre}, models {Devil Doll, Don Hendrie}, a black earth relation of The Dracula Tour {highly recommended}, delicious Vampire Wine, a biographical essay on Tepes by Warlock Nocturnum, and even a fictional interview with the man himself!

Most notable in My estimation is the compelling statement from Vlad The Just by Magister Lang {suitable for framing, in My opinion}, with splendid photographs of Lang's Vlad statue from Magus Gilmore, as well as an interview with Magister Lang.

For those who appreciate the darkly opulent eroticism of Vampira, Morticia Addams, Elvira, and Lily Munster, we have succulent fetish models richly spicing up the issue throughout {Devil Doll, Red Vamp, Vampire Wear}. The delightfully gloomy photography of Madame Webb, inclusive of somber natural locations, and Victorian total environments with their living and ever-living inhabitants.

With a slick magazine presentation filled to the brim within its 66+ pages, also included are elegant advertisements to the fine products of Scapegoat Publishing, Femaledictions, Headless Historicals, Nox Arcana, and Le'Rue Delashay.

The Ninth Gate is a publication that The Addams Family and The Munsters would subscribe to, and with an uplifted glass of black flame absinthe, is an absolute pleasure for The Blackthorne Manor to possess. [the9thgate.com]

The Ninth Gate II
{Walpurgisnacht XLII A.S.}

The Ninth Gate opens with pieces on Baphomet by Warlock Corvis Nocturnum, 'Satanic Altar Tools' by Bill M., followed by interviews with Black Metal band Shroud, and Dark Horizon Records company owner Typhus; there are art gallery features by artists Storm and Strephon Taylor; a pleasing spotlight on a deliciously-exquisite {brunette in this expose'} fetish model Bianca Beauchamp; a focus on publisher Old Nick Magazine; the gates close with salaciously-thoughtful essay 'The Intrinsic Decadence' by Mikael Walach, an analysis on the innate Satanic drive towards erotica.

Also included are Multimedia reviews on Magus Gilmore's superlative Threnody For Humanity CD, and book reviews of Lucifer Rising and Lords of Chaos.

Additionally, there are sinister product referrals to Scapegoat Publishing, Radio Free Satan, the fine arts and crafts of Blackthorne Productions, Femaledictions, Le'Rue Delashay, Artistic Devil, Diabolic Publications, Headless Historicals, and Monolith Graphics featuring the splendid musick of Nox Arcana, and more.

With shadowy cover art featuring Warlock Nocturnum's rendition of Warlock Netherworld's Baphomet design, The Ninth Gate unleashes yet another plethora of highly recommended infernal delights.

Dark Somewhere
A Magazine of Dark Fiction
XLIII A.S. Issue #2. $5 U.S. / $7 International. 44 pages.

Dark Somewhere magazine presents five morbid tales of horror fantasy from various authors including Warlock Hernandez, Michael Silva himself, and this writer, plunging the depths of the carnal, erotic, the feral, the chthonic, and the mystical.

Each darkly well-descriptive story is accompanied by an impressive rendering of the tale told by the expert pen of Mr. Silva, creating a veritable "Lovecraftian Journal" of thrilling terrors perfect for a dark stormy night.

Art within features draconian forms in flight, a Sorcerer coalescing with an old one from the stygian leagues, a plethora of salacious demonic creatures, a humanimalistic warrior, and generously curvacious succubi throughout.

Filled with suspense, thrilling escapades, and concupiscent contemplation, Dark Somewhere magazine is aesthetically as well as literarily pleasing - a sheer pleasure to aphotically enjoy. [boltofthegoat.com]

S Magazine
{Volume 3, 2007. Published by editors Priestess Kim Rice and Witch Josephine Seven}

None other than Minnie Castavet graces the cover of issue 3 of S magazine, a really wonderful Satanic lifestyle journal, and in full color, no less, in vivid laser-print quality. I particularly enjoy the Satanic Homemaker of the Year contest with some of My favorite fetishistic women {I

wonder if Samantha Stevens was also in the running?}.

Herein is filled with many imaginative recipes for various dark cuisines, to gardening, total environments, pets, incense-making and historicity, makeup tips, an interview with a lounge act, incisive essays on technology {by this author} and philosophical contemplation, and the hilarious mailbag section! Plus much more in this elegant and generous 66 page comb-bound compendium.

S Magazine is a veritable 'Satanic Martha Stewart' publication optimally recommended for all things dealing with The Satanist's Lair. Indeed, the very fact that this publication even exists is further testament that we are absolutely in full 'swing' within The Age of Fire. [s-magazine.com]

Infernus
{V. VIII, Spring Equinox XLIII A.S., 24 pp.}

"The Voice of Satanism in Portugal."

Infernus VIII, Spring Equinox XLIII A.S.From Satan's Helloutro, who also brought us the Portuguese translation of The Satanic Bible, comes Infernus magazine, a beautifully-done Portuguese Satanic publication featuring essays on Carducci {including his distinguished poem Inno A Satana}, Atheism fundamentals, Surrealism, remarkable cover art "Don't Fear" by Simon, an art piece by D. Blackthorne, an interview with band Teatro Satanico {"Satanic Theater"}, aesthetic individualism, an analysis of amateur painting styles, plus much more.

Being that Satanism spans all languages and cultures worldwide {also see 'The Infernal Names' as an indication}, one can truly appreciate this international expression of our philosophy. Well done! Hail Satan! [apsatanismo.org]

Born of The Night
2008 c.e. Gothic Fantasy Calendar

A splendid collection of Gothic images rendered by Joseph Vargo, features full page glossy prints of these marvelously gloomy portraits birthed from the dark subconscious. Dates detail infamous events and individuals of grim historical note with a marble background and glowing numerals, also illustrating moon phases, seasonal equinoxes, solstices, and even astrological signs, if so inclined. Of course, at any point herein one may etch their own events of

significance, and it is even better if one possesses a certain sigil stamp to accentuate them as desired.

This '2008' edition includes supplementary inlets per month as well, providing even more aesthetic gratification to compliment one's observance and overall Lair.

Filled with phantoms, demons, vampires, gargoyles, strange creatures, wraiths, Sorcerers and Witches, the Born of The Night Calendar is sure to delight the senses for monthly Halloweens throughout the year.

Giger Calendar 2008 c.e.
Morpheus Gallery

Giger Calendar 2008 c.e.Dare you venture into Giger's Satanic World of nether-wordly creatures and Hellish landscapes? A place which brings comfort and inspiration, familiarity and contemplation... plunge the depths of The Abyss, open the gates to the dark subconscious and dwell in twelve supreme months of infernal meditation upon these legendary masterpieces.

* Contents:

Untitled {For Graw}, ELP II, Hieroglyphics {Work No. 385} [1], LI Sculpt, Birthmachine [2], Monsters of Rock [3], Magus [4], Landscape XXIII, Tourist VII [5], SIL {Detail} [6], Passagen, Aleph [7].

The glossy black Giger Calendar also includes special notes of observation, infamous dates and individuals of remembrance, a biography including a diabolically-stylized portrait of The Artist, photos of the Giger Bar & Museum H.R. Giger in Switzerland, along with monthly quotes from historical artists, writers, philosophers, and occultists.

Giger has the amazing capability to interpret mythological concepts in his own lambent artistic style, utilizing tradition, imagination, and improvisation to manifest a unique iconoclastic vision. It is truly a pleasure to display this veritable portfolio in The Blackthorne Lair.

_____
* Here I shall describe some of the more remarkable presentations from this edition in My estimation:

[1] In Egyptian metaphorical mythology, Nuit provides the framework of the universe, with a pharaoh ascending into the ether,

accompanied by the egg of transformation / regeneration.

[2] A clever depiction of both insemination via this phallic metal instrument / chamber of lust, combined with a likely depiction of the birth canal. Read: "Love Gun".

[3] A more or less 'untraditional' work by Giger, employing vibrant color combinations into an amalgam of amorphous images, faces and forms.

[4] A definite top favorite. depicting an adept and his thought forms, detailing highly symbolically descriptive processes of Magical practice.

[5] Some of his more bio-mechanic work, featuring android-like creatures out for a perusal.

[6] A dream-like morbid lady in metallic skeletal bio-mechanoid motif.

[7] Carries an encompassing erotic element with yoni and lingam displayed within the menagerie, seemingly signifying sexual magic.

Spechtreum
Filmography Reviews

KNIGHT RIDER

"A young man set on revenge. His partner... an indestructible car. .... A lone crusader in a dangerous world....the world of....the Knight Rider ..."

Knight Rider has remained a favored presentation of Mine ever since I became aware of it as a Dracling, and it is no wonder it held a natural attraction, considering that upon analysis, it is obviously replete with Satanic principles throughout!

KITT ['Knight Industries Two-Thousand'; The Infernal Machine]

Not only is KITT a manifestation of Artificial Intelligence, which we are major proponents of, from the aesthetics demonstrating The Command to Look {The Lighthouse Effect}, but also the fact that it was built for a governmental weapons plan called 'Promethius', seems a very obvious contemplation, as Promethius is another iconic representation of the Satanic, and a very appropriate one.

In the Greek myth, the iconoclastic Promethius brought the flame of life and forbidden knowledge to mankind, with a myriad of cultural correlations.

In the latest version, "KITT 3000" is a Mustang, quite a beautiful model,

looking much more "muscle car" in this production, rather than the sleek Trans-Am of the KITT 2000, which still remains in first place for My taste, yet I would still not hesitate to operate either nonetheless. Instead of the uni-strobe coursing all the way from one end of the visor to the other, it is comprised of two side by side, which has a certain appeal, although the single strobe is more preferential in My observation, rather like a Cylon from Battlestar Galactica.

In its interactive interface, the only real difference seems to be that KITT has an accompanying visual screen which can now bring up images and graphs to accompany the information related. KITT can also morph into other models by modifying the molecular structure of the hulk surface.

KITT's disposition is quite Spockian, although [he] seems to eventually develop a sense of empathy.

Michael Knight

I have always found Michael Knight to be very Batman / Bruce Wayne like. Son of the original by the same name, Mike Jr. is also an Army Ranger {whereas Batman is a Ninja, and Knight Sr., a former Cop}, although every bit as carnal and roguish as The Hoff's characterization. At once a scoundrel and a gentleman, a lover and a fighter, displaying a perfect synthesis of the two.

Whether in a turtleneck, leather jacket, or suit and tie, Knight is a sharp dresser, certainly not displaying a lack of aesthetics. Besides being skilled in the technical processes of operating and driving KITT, he is well trained in the Martial Arts.

Knight and KITT compliment each other very well - for besides being partners, it could be analyzed that they both represent a Yin-Yang dynamic, both halves of the cerebrum fused into one entity; KITT is the analytical, while Knight being human, expresses the more passionate / emotional.

Overview

Knight Rider movie: When KITT's designer Charles Graiman's life is threatened, a new Knight Rider must be found, discovering him in Michael Knight's estranged son by the same name. To amend a debt and save his friend from some thugs, Michael leaves to gamble up the money owed in Sin City, but when his former girlfriend appears with KITT seeking his help while being stalked by Black Hawk agents, Knight instinctually steps forth, quickly acclimating to the situation, and to KITT. The chase ensues through dangerous canyons until the final

confrontation at a Bates' Motel-like location, amidst a grove of weeping willows, where his mother meets her unfortunate demise. After outsmarting the Black Hawk agents, he is asked to assume his new role, at first declining, but after meeting his father Knight Sr. {The Hoff!} at the funeral, his 'destiny' seems clear, and Knight Rider rides again...

The plot is quite similar to that of the 'Knight of The Phoenix' pilot episode. However, I found this latest presentation to be about average, but definitely superior to the forgettable "Team Knight Rider" in My opinion, but as is often the case, sequels and remakes do not surpass the original. It does have a tendency to grow on one, however. We shall have to see what develops.

White Zombie

{1932 c.e. Directed by Victor Halperin. Written by Garnett Weston. Starring Bela Lugosi, Madge Bellamy, Joseph Cawthorn, Robert Frazer, John Harron, Brandon Hurst, George Burr Macannan, Frederick Peters, Annette Stone, John Printz, Dan Crimmins, Claude Morgan, John Fergusson, Velma Gresham. Genre: Horror.}

Gaze into the eyes of The Warlock...

Beautiful Madeleine Short and her fiancee' Neil Parker travel the twisting roads of Haiti to acquaintance Charles Beaumont's plantation in a cortege' to be wed, when they briefly meet one Mr. Legendre {Lugosi} along the way, who absconds with her scarf, a remnant of her person, and the horror begins. The carriage driver regails them with the local legends of zombies, and when a group of these living dead amble about Legendre down from the black hills, they are struck with an uneasy terror and speedily make their way to Beaumont's plantation, where they are met by a pipe-smoking Dr. Bruner.

However, seems the cleverly traitorous Beaumont essentially made a deal with The Devil by employing the necromantic services of Legendre, to possess Madeleine for his very own zombie love slave. But in order to achieve this end, she must 'die' first, or enter into a narcoleptic coma with her mind in a spell.

Beaumont gets to see the secret caverns where Legendre keeps his native slaving zombies at the creeking mill reminiscent of the proles from Metropolis, and is also introduced to Legendre's various primary zombies. There's Chauvin the executioner {who almost executed Legendre}, a large monster of a man with an intimidating glare; Ledot, Legendre's former instructor still in ceremonial attire; Von

Gelder, the former tyrrannical dictator of the isle; and Silver the zombie butler.

Quite remarkably, Legendre works his dark art by fashioning a waxen fetish figure carved right from a candle, wrapped in her scarf, and improvisationally burns it in a lantern's flame. Here is where Lugosi gestures that infamous hand gesticulation to gain control of her consciousness.

Meanwhile, Parker plunges into despair and becomes enebriated at a local bar, eventually stumbling over to her grave while she is being extracted by Legendre and his zombies. Upon discovering her body missing, he screams in anguish. Now seeking the aid of Dr. Bruner {who really should invest in a lighter}, a sort of Van-Helsing type, he becomes elucidated about the zombie tales, and prepares to visit Legendre at his magnificent cliff-side castle.

When Beaumont is taken aback by Madeleine's condition, recognizing no personality behind her blank stare, he regrets his decision and begs Legendre to reverse her somnambulism, to his lethal misfortune. Now it is he who ingests the zombie powder, while Legendre ghoulishly savors each moment of his degeneration, even fashioning the effigie right in front of him - the only one among all the zombies who actually realizes what is happening to him.

For a brief moment, Madeleine seemingly recognizes Beaumont through the haze, but Legendre regains control. Unfortunately, while she walks outside, Beaumont summons one last vestige of effort and takes Legendre with him over the cliff's edge, followed by his other zombies*. The spell is broken, and the fiancee's are reunited. Lesson: always leave someone in charge of whomever is in the next room!

Subsequent to Dracula, Lugosi played a remarkable role with this remarkable character, which also remains an inspirational model of deportment and determination. A veritable 'devil as a gentleman'.

White Zombie is repleat with splendid camera angles {inclusive of mesmerizing close-ups}, lambent and contrasting lighting techniques, morbid, shadowy sets, striking vistas, and memorable scenes sure to secure a treasured spot in one's collection, as well as in one's mind. [5/5].

---

* Here one will recognize a scene from Speak of The Devil during 'Battle Hymn of The Apocalypse' wherein during the inunciation of "...let the zombies grope for light...", the bodies plunge over the edge.

H P. Lovecraft's

DAGON

{XXXVI A.S. Based on short stories "Dagon" and "The Shadow Over Innsmouth" by H. P. Lovecraft. Directed by Stuart Gordon. Screenplay by Dennis Paoli. Starring Ezra Godden, Francisco Rabal, Raquel Meroño,, Macarena Gómez, Brendan Price, Birgit Bofarull, Uxía Blanco, Ferran Lahoz. Made in Spain. Genre: Horror.}

"Dagon - Philistine avenging devil of the sea." ~ The Satanic Bible.

Paul Marsh, his girlfriend Barbara, and another couple {one of whom doesn't make it} are shipwrecked by a mysterious storm, becoming stranded in a dank Spanish town named "Imboca" {what would have been "Innsmouth"}, populated by transmutating barely human amphibious creatures.

When his companions disappear, he learns the truth of this place from "Ezequiel", an elderly vagrant who relates that the strange occupants are actually cultists who worship the Cthulhu-like Dagon, and have long since turned the local Catholic Church {whose then-resident priest was slain} into one of this sea god. This yields to highly dramatic scenes of transition featuring a High Priest taking control of the town. Their emblem resembles a subaqueous "all-seeing eye" which replaces smashed christian icons.

Marsh is pursued by the tentacle-limbed zombie-like inhabitants through one suspenseful situation to the next, where he eventually discovers human skin hanging from hooks, other mutant creatures, and a really enchantingly beautiful mermaid named Uxia {the delicious Macarena Gomez} pining for his amorous attention. Throughout this tale, it seems he had oneiromantically forseen glimpses of this entire adventure in his dreams, from the alien symbols to this beauty.

He, Barbara, and Ezequiel eventually find themselves about to be sacrificed to the hungry Dagon, until Marsh is rescued by this superb mermaid, who desires him for her own. Turns out Uxia is the High Priestess, attired in glorious ceremonial vestments, lifting an impressive spinal dagger, uttering the invocation "IA! IA! Cthulhu F'Thag'n" phrase ubiquitous in the Lovecraftian mythos. At the ceremony, the black robed High Priest comes forth, who has since evolved into the personafication of Cthulhu will an octopus head and tentacles about the mouth.

Ezequiel is killed, and Barbara is lowered into a well-like pit to feed the aquatic beast. In the end, despite the self-immolation of Marsh, the Dagonites actually prevail, as he essentially sheds his skin to join the sublime Uxia when he realizes he is actually one of them.

Beginning in a lightmare, Dagon concludes in a nightmarish purging. With minimal gore, some brief CGI, and gloomy environments, this is a thrilling, and very dark film with a refreshing twist, sans the typical duality and plot outcome common in most cult / monster movies, where the protagonist was formally his own antagonist, who experiences realization and acceptance of his true nature. [4/5]

The Manitou

{XII A.S. Directed by William Girdler. Written by Jon Cider, William Girdler. Starring Tony Curtis, Michael Ansara, Susan Strasberg, Burgess Meredith, Felix Silla. Genre: Horror}

"Manitou: a supernatural being that controls nature; a spirit, deity, or object that possesses supernatural power." - American Heritage Dictionary.

When a fetus grows on the back of his girlfriend's neck, it is up to Harry Erskine, a psychic scheisster, to find help for her. Seems he began to meddle in certain occult practices that he could not handle, and so his problems surmount, amusingly displayed when an elderly client is possessed and floats out the door and tumbles down the stairs. Despite all attempts to help her condition using "white man's medicine", he realizes he must consult alternative methods including a seance where an "evil spirit" manifests as a black head rising from the table.

While researching, he finds the name of professor Dr. Snow {Burgess Meredith} who recommends he fight fire with fire, leading him to a reservation where he meets reticent Medicine Man John Singing Rock, who takes on the challenge for a generous donation to the Native American education fund and some tobacco. When he discovers the fetus is the reincarnation of a legendary powerful shaman named Misquamacus {played by Felix "Cousin Itt" Silla and Joe Gieb}, his reticence grows but nonetheless decides to attempt a fight, despite a warning by Misquamacus to not help the palefaces. Every effort is met with defeat as Misquamacus summons everything from a lizard demon, the zombified body of a dead orderly, to the elements themselves, transforming the floor level into a veritable cave. Unfortunately, Misquamacus is deformed and diminuative due to profuse X-radiation while attempting to decipher the mysterious growth.

When John Singing Rick explains that all things have a manitou, even seemingly inanimate objects, and when all else fails, Harry conceives of an idea to use the manitous of all the hospital's computers, hoping to amass their combined energy to combat Misquamacus, who at that point has summoned forth "The Devourer", a supposed equivalent to The Devil, which leads to a surprisingly impressive phantasmagoric ending.

With subtle shades of Koyaanisqatsi, the plot seems to convey a message of the progression of technology at odds with the natural world, although in the end, a cooperative balance can be found. [4/5]

"Mighty be the powers of the old medicine man
Whispers of his rain dance flow across the desert sands Guardian of the elder spirit summoning the storm Awaiting his arrival, Manitou of flesh is born..."~ 'Manitou' by Venom; At War With Satan.

When Good Ghouls Go Bad

{XXXVI A.S. Written by R.L. Stine. Directed by Patrick Read Johnson. Starring Christopher Lloyd, Tom Amandes, Roy Billing, Brittany Byrnes, Brendan McCarthy. Genre: Thriller}

From Goosebumps' author R.L. Stine comes this delightful Halloween-themed tale, both charming and evocatively enjoyable:

Founded by the delightfully eccentric "Uncle" Fred Walker, Walker Falls has not seen a Halloween for years because of a so-called "curse" placed upon it by one "Curtis Danko" {obvious 'Donnie Darko' influenced nomenclature}, labeled the town "weirdo" for his preference to dress in black, and express his imagination with monsters, and scenes of a world gone mad. His creativity is clearly envied by others, and thus, they react in fearful passive-aggressive manners which are no less than despicable, displaying their inferior and odious ill-natures.

So once when the art class project was to sculpt a depiction of one's hero*, the school bully and cronies lock him in the incinerator as a prank. He actually resembles Edward Scissorhands while sculpting.

Urban Legend: He refused for anyone to see his project, guarding it from all during the day. He returns at night to work on it in private. Next one morning, when Mike Kankel walks into the classroom, he notices

something is wrong, and discovers Danko's ashes in the incinerator with his statue, with a forboding message written in the ashes, that if the town celebrates Halloween, he will return and face his wrath:

"If you ever have another Halloween again, I will return and destroy you all!"

Kankel pretends at blindness, claiming that the statue is so terrible that no one should look upon it as if made by someone counceled by The Devil, , lest they go blind, or head explode, or even turn to stone, a-la Medusa's glare. So the ashes and statue are sealed within a crypt with nicely arranged cob-webbed chains.

Factuality: After a teasing session, Danko is incarcerated in the incinerator to be left until the following morning. Unfortunately, an absent-minded janitor accidentally taps the 'on' button, immolating Danko. Terrified of being blamed for his murder, he writes the warning in the ashes himself and claims that looking upon the statue blinded him for three days. It was later confessed that now Coach Kankel did it because funds were being directed into the fine arts at the school instead of sports activities.

'Uncle' Walker's grandson Danny arrives from Chicago to attend this new school, and is bullied by Kankel's son and his moronic hench boy. Despite this, he befriends Dayna who shows him marvelous secrets within Danko's haunted house, where, unbeknownst to the a-dolt towns people, the Magic of Halloween has been preserved - skeletons, skulls, demons, monsters, ghouls, bats, spiders, ghosts, zombies, witches, are all here in this abandoned mansion to be enjoyed in secret by the towns children**.

When Danny's business-minded father James suggests the town hold a "Spooktacular" Halloween celebration at a town meeting, the residents go bananas with fear, especially when time and time again, Halloween decorations begin mysteriously appearing about. James Walker seeks to re-open Walker Chocolates {also founded by nucleus Uncle Walker, in a Willy Wonka vein}, with the help of soon-arriving German Businessmen, and the support of the towns people.

Uncle Walker is quite a character, who listens to his Hammond Organ recordings on his jukebox, building elaborate tracks for his hot wheels, surrounded by amusing nick knacks, while attired in various playful outfits. He serves as a true father for Danny, since his dad is virtually un-present in the goings-on of his life. Someone who could actually offer the wisdom of experience as well as be a playmate and friend. Also

mentionable is the sage wisdom imparted to Danny about the Magic of Halloween...

So when he apparently dies from a bash on the head by a falling pumpkin from a veritable pumpkin mountain pile which strangely appears in the town square, his heart is broken until he later returns as a zombie to help him place Danko's statue in its rightful place. In the meantime, several amusing circumstances unfold including the appearence of 'Cheesy The Clown' {quite a lokian depiction}, and Uncle Walker retrieving his runaway hand, a-la Thing {especially humorous considering Christopher Lloyd wonderfully portrayed Uncle Fester in treasured films 'The Addams Family' & 'Addams Family Values'}.

When Danko returns from the grave with green-glowing eyes in skeletal form, who along with various other zombies, at the secret Halloween dance, all is finally set to balance as Halloween is restored, after a shameful spectacle and confession by Coach Kankel, the statue is finally seen, which provides for quite a surprise, followed by a moving ending scene and narration. [5/5]

_____

* Interesting to note that I actually sculpted a statue for art class of a Baphomet-headed Satan in a robe wearing a pentagram medallion, holding a sword in one hand and signifying The Cornu with the other. To My surprise, Sgt. Randy Emon was notified, who took photos of it for his occult portfolio.
** It can be observed that the mansion is also a metaphor for the subconscious accumulation of archetypal images of fear and memento moris, waiting to be released and celebrated. To deny them only causes an unbalanced psyche.

Satanic Panic Archive

Exposing The Satanic Web
1990 c.e. Dave Roever Ministries

Retrospective christinsanity. Cosmopolitan divine madness. It is interesting to observe the types described therein their own dualistic paradigm - all sheeple, whether white or black by whatever name/s used, just all want to cluster and worship some type of external "god" delusion together. These nuts are classified as devil-worshippers, not Satanists, and they can have them.

This christian propaganda may just be the more disturbing of the lot, considering some of the relations made by those who supposedly "remembered" being victimized as children, but as we unfortunately know now, these were actually fictional projections from psycho-the-rapists upon their patients, indoctrinating them with all manner of paranoia and false memory scenarios in order to sustain them in the business of fear, as well as justify their misdirected sense of masochism, and pretentious Crusader Syndrome.

This "documentary", and some others like it, was released briefly prior to the FBI's findings that these massive cult allegations were proven false, and thus slipped into obscurity when the religious enterprise could no longer take advantage of this latest cultural fear-trend.

The man claiming to have been a former "Satanic High Priest" is nonsense. That loser was a self-admitted druggie, relishing in the meager attention granted by the undiscriminating media of the time, then fabricating lurid tales of intoxicated hysteria. The woman attempting to read some sort of meaning into the Slayer cover art to bolster her claims of a "Satanic Conspiracy" {which of course was proven false by the FBI} is quite amusing as well. Anyone wanting to know anything about Satanism, or any other subject for that matter, should look to actual literature, and not music intended for pure theatrical entertainment. Yet this was the degree of blindlight lunacy and insecurity exhibited during the Satanic Panic, a seemingly resurgent sub-mentality from the 'witch' trials.

SINEMÆROTICA

The Maddams Family

{XXVIII A.S. Directed by Herschel Savage. Starring Ona Zee, Mike Horner, Charisma, Deidre Holland, Kim Angeli, Ron Jeremy, Jon Dough. Genre: Sinemaerotica, Comedy, Parody. Rated: XXX. Wicked Pictures. 69 minutes}

"They're creepy, but more horny. They'll do you in the morning. Each other they're adoring, the Maddam's Family. The men are hung like horses. They don't need back up forces. They always cum in quartses, the Maddam's Family. She's Sweet, He's neat, Feel the heat. So when you need some lovin, or some cushion for your shovin, we got what you've been wanting, the Maddam's Family. "

CAST ANALYSIS

Based on The Addams Family, the characters herein are amusingly renamed, albeit rather predictably vulgar:

Gomez is "Cortez" {probably the best cast; Mike Horner looks like a Spaniard and is aptly named after the legendary foremost Conquistadore}, Morticia is "Horticia" {Ona Zee in a bad wig with bangs, yet still very succulent; while Morticia seemed to be about a 5 o'clock on the Personality Synthesizer Clock, Zee's frame is more of a 7 o'clock}, Cousin Itt is "Cousin Tit" {the generously-busted 'Charisma' with hair pulled down over her face while wearing sunglasses}, Uncle Fester is "Pester" {Ron Jeremy in bald cap and hooded robe with a moustache; obviously, Fester is clean-shaven and wears a cassok}, Wednesday is "Tuesday" {a cute Kim Angeli; NOT a daughter, but the 18 y.o. niece, or "kissing cousin", as it were}, Thing is "Thingie" {a female hand, more akin to Lady Fingers herein}, and Lurch is "Crotch" {this actually works well with a groaning Jon Dough in zombie-like make-up}. Fortunately, there are no versions of Grandmama or Pugsley, which probably would have proven too disturbing.

PLOT

Seems The Maddams Family are facing possible financial hardship because peace has broken out across the world, which lends to the conjecture that they profit from warfare, among other things, a-la Basil Zaharoff as "agents provocateurs".

Being exclusive individuals who find general herd interaction frustrating and intolerable, they must divulge a method to work from home. Their brainstorming results in deciding to enter the erotica biz and run an elegant brothel from the Victorian Manse, but first, they must sexercise to gain sexperience, and diligently begin practicing upon each other at every opportunity.

To the tune of her French enunciations, Cortez and Horticia passionately indulge in each other in the bedroom which features gloomy surroundings and a stained glass window; shedding her form-fitting dress, she reveals alluring black lingerie while Cortez savors and plunges into her sumptuously. Cousin Tit and Tuesday have a delightful romp; the galavanting Cousin Tit* initiates an intense orgasm in the playfully coy Tuesday, who claims to have never experienced that degree of pleasure before; a salacious Cortez subsequently enjoys nubile Tuesday as well; later, a virginal Uncle Pester and Tit cavort in the garden, while she is very well surprised and pleased by the proportions of his appendage {"Who knew what was beneath that robe?"}; and finally, a blond house

inspector arrives to *ass*ess the property while accompanied by Horticia, discover Crotch receiving a helping hand from Thingie, when they decide to converge upon the situation as well, which lasts a good 15 minutes or so, in various enjoyable positions, with Crotch periodically uttering his characteristic groan from time to time.

Other scenes include Cortez fencing with Crotch in the courtyard, and towards the end, Horticia clipping roses. Music is jaunty, ranging from a customized variant on the Addams Family theme, to the classically 'spooky' Beethoven's Fifth, and even a couple of instances of black noise, believe it or not.

In the end, the business of pleasure is a success, and The Maddams Family prevail by their resourcefulness, truly utilizing their best assets. [4/5]

Addendum

For one who has long since appreciated, and even personified The Addams Family in many respects, I have to admit that I was somewhat taken aback by this when I first became aware of its existence around the time when the first movie was released as I perused a video store. It almost seemed 'sacriligeous', yet still, there was something quite compelling about a proposed erotic version of these characters that was nestled in the back of My mind - after all, Morticia Addams and the fetishistic like do hold quite an obvious prurient appeal, what with her tight black dress and long black hair, and very well serves as an E.C.I. So when I recently had the opportunity to view this presentation, I was curious to survey what had been created. Plus, with some of the recent wonderfully Satantric artwork created by Isabel Samaras in this vain, it held even more of an attraction.

Having the entire original series collection, the films {even the underwhelming "Reunion"}, the charming Halloween special, along with various other collectables, the parody is a must for those who can appreciate such eccentrically odd comedic sinemaerotica.

---

* Humorously appropriate, considering in The Addams Family series, Cousin It is known as quite the playboy.

Malefik Musick
Discography Reviews

Acheron
Rites of The Black Mass
{XLIII A.S. Dying Music Records. Vocals, Bass, Rhythm Guitar: Vincent Crowley; Pete Slate: Lead Guitar; James Strauss: Drums; Magus Peter H. Gilmore: Introductory Narrations. Genre: Metal / Symphonic}

Acheron: Rites of The Black MassWith impressive new album art, featuring The Prince of Darkness enthroned and accompanied by a couple of succubi and serpents in an appropriately Hellish environment, the re-release of Rites of The Black Mass is still complete with introductory orchestral narrations by Magus Gilmore, with songs featuring genuine litany from Dr. LaVey's The Satanic Rituals' cathartically theatrical Le Messe Noir, making this opus unique by itself, but for those who appreciate the Blackest of Metal musick straight from The Pit, this remains a barely comparable unleashing, casting an evocatively embracing shadow of formative daemonic evilution.

A CD booklet with lyrics is also included, which the previous circa XXXI A.S. did not include {one had to actually request it from The Order of The Evil Eye, due to the explicitly intense blasphemous lyrics, which was quite pioneering in the latter phase of The Satanic Panic}, threatening and seemingly succeeding in pulling the fetters of mythological heaven down, with some new band photos added as well; and quite pleasingly, I received an autographed copy from Mr. Crowley himself. Sound is excellent, if not even enhanced.

So even if you still possess the original CD, cassette, or vinyl, this one is definitely worth acquiring if just for the artistry for your salacious contemplation, and the fact that demos and pre-demos for ROTBM are graciously included herein. If you have never heard, and otherwise desired to experience this previously-hard to find musickal tribute to the Luciferian rebellious liberation of The Black Mass, now is your chance to sign the pact!

"666"

Acherontas
Tat Tvam Asi {Universal Omniscience} {XLI A.S. Zyklon-B Productions. Genre: Orchestral. Metal. 47.6 minutes}

Focusing on the philosophies of The Temple of The Vampire, this elitist Satanic Vampire band returns to take your mind into a swirling vortex of etheric predation and immortal contemplation.

I. Alfa: Genesis {instrumental}, II. Tat Tvam Asi, III. Soma Elixir Of The Ancient Ones, IV. Kali-Yuga, V. Sophia {instrumental}, VI. The Final Harvest, VII. The Dreamer, VIII. Omega: The Seal Of The Dragon

The ritualistic opus begins with the sublime Alfa: Genesis, a beautifully melancholy violin sonata layered to compliment the two inter-plays. Launching into entropic sonic permutations with a vocal and musickal style reminiscent of Emperor, combined with deeply-demonic invocative narratives spoken in both Greek and English, casting images of a dark pagan history with a modern Black Metal expression.

Particularly enjoyable are the inclusions of enchanting succubus Weisses Blut's necrogasmically passionate voice {Kali-Yuga} in contrast with Acherontas' overall pervasive bestial echoings, as if resounding across space and timelessness, descending from mountains and through the shadowy forests of Hellas.

The introspective Sophia offers a hypnotically lachrymose piano sonata, blending into the prognosticating The Final Harvest which wonderfully mixes the epic Metal with a haunting instrumental orchestration, and mirthful spectral whisperings. The Dreamer begins with a frantic organ, slipping into the dark electrical percolations again, amidst gloomy ceremonial enunciations of doom or self-salvation. To the sounds of the purifying bell, the Vampiric ritual concludes with an ecstatic Omega: The Seal of The Dragon.

Through the inter-dimensional looking glass, the booklet unleashes sepia visions with a lucid dream style, featuring Baphomet and The Winged Skull of Ur, blending into spectacles of our origins as the alien-predators elite.

Hail Baphomet! Hail Tiamat! Hail Satan!

5/5

The Blackthorne Theatre
geocities.com/dblackthorne/BlackthorneTheatre

SINEMæROTICA

Satanic Sickies

{VII/XIX/XLI A.S. Alpha Blue Archives. Genre: Sinemaerotica}

KundalingamSatanic Sickies is an amusing archival compendium of fictional sinemaerotic productions from the 70's & 80's with occult and demonic themes intended for adult entertainment, and do not display actual Satanic practices in all respects, although there are many obvious influences displayed deriving from The Satanic Bible & The Satanic Rituals books, Satanis: The Devil's Mass documentary, and Dr. LaVey's aesthetic persona.

Just to be clear, consider the following statements from The Satanic Bible:

"Under no circumstances would a Satanist sacrifice any animal or baby!" {TSB; 'On The Choice of A Human Sacrifice', page 89}

"Satanism does not advocate rape, child molesting, sexual defilement of animals, or any other form of sexual activity which entails the participation of those who are unwilling or whose innocence or naiveté' would allow them to be intimidated or misguided into doing something against their wishes." {TSB; 'Satanic Sex', page 70}

Discriminate with care, sin well, and have fun!

Box Set 2

The front cover features a rendition of Dr. Anton Szandor LaVey standing before a Baphomet accompanied by Togare, a female nude altar holding a skull {in a similar pose to that of Jayne Mansfield}, a succubus emerging from a coffin a-la 'L'Air Epais' {see book: The Satanic Rituals}, The Golden Gate Bridge, a wrecked automobile, seemingly detailing the incident with the accursed Sam Brody, all amidst the hell fires of Lust.

Back Cover Description: "Includes bonus loops: Witch Sabbath Hexensabbat, Lucifer's Lust & more! Alpha Blue Proudly Presents this premier package of Satanic, vampire and Witchcraft Sex Films from the 70's! Seekers of the bizarre and obscure will not be disappointed with this collection that highlights the 1970's pre-occupation with Occult themes! Sometimes shocking, hilarious and always entertaining these films include themes of ritual sacrifice, mutilation, sex orgies, satanic possession & exorcism, vampirism & bloodsucking, haunted mansions, necrophilia, devil-worship and much more! FULL LENGTH FEATURE FILM TITLES INCLUDE: DEVIL INSIDE HER, SEDUCTION OF AMY, DEVIL'S DUE, SORCERESS, SUCKULA, LAST STEP DOWN, SATAN'S SEX SLAVES, BLUE VOODOO, SEXORCIST DEVIL, HOTTER THAN HELL, NIGHT OF THE WARLOCK, MADAM SATAN."

Disc I

Devil Inside Her

{XI A.S. A.K.A. "Metamorphosis". Taurus Productions. Written & Directed by Zebedy Colt. Produced by Jason West. Starring Jody Maxwell, Terri Hall, Dean Tait, Rod Dumont. 69 minutes.}

Note: In an almost "Aristocrats" manner, this film seems to want to be as shocking as possible, trampling taboos left and right, and it does manage to be disturbing from time to time. Expressing the dualistic Judeo-Christian superstitious legends of antiquity, it manages to pull up just about every hysterical notion leveled against proposed diabolists to frighten their congregations firmly into church pews. Besides being propaganda, these tales not only provided propaganda for Catholic and Protestant churches, but also served as a convenient venue with which to express their own desperately repressed projections.]

Set in repressively Puritanical 1826 New England, Joseph {who resembles "Rocky" from RHPS} and Faith are just a couple in love, but he is also desired by her sister Hope, who will do anything to attain his affections, including making a deal with The Devil, if that's what it takes. But the rift has already begun when they are caught kissing by 'father', who whips Faith within an inch of her life, admonishing that she stand naked before "God" and read the bible, after calling her a harlot, and he a lecher.

Hope's request does not go unheeded, while agonizing in the forest, The Devil proclaims "Don't give up, 'Hope'", and appears as a hirsute, lascivious man with an elongated appendage in make-up that could be a cross between King Diamond's and Gene Simmons', with slicked hair forming a widow's peak and horns, wearing nothing but a cape, studded gauntlets, collar, and boots. Overall, resembling what could be a demonic Frank-N-Furter. Transforming into the form of Joseph, and to her self-deceptive trepidation, he takes Faith into the pinnacles of ecstasy.

Hope visits the village Witch at her hovel for advice, a pocked hag of a woman who mixes up a potion of love for her {containing some of the classical disgusting Shakespearian ingredients such as "bat's eyes", "lizard's tongue", "the puss from a dying virgin", "bone dust of a pilgrim lecher", "the menstrual fluid of a Persian Harlot", "the sweat of a goat", "the blood of a fresh-killed toad", and the final ingredient that makes it all work, the "love juice of Nicodemus" {she turns her parrot into a "wood sprite", a salacious man with no seed of his own, but is filled with a collection of that sove "spilled by naughty disobedient boys"}, which must be drawn from "the human snake that grows to fill the void", which lets forth its bounty into the bowl. After she leaves with a vial of the potion {in which she will "see her lover in her own eyes"; so of course, The Devil later takes advantage of this}, He then emerges wherein the crone collects her reward from his thorn.

In the process, she utters some zingers like,

"Is it not the evil in the world that makes good seem duller than it is? That frightened fathers send dry girls to seek My kind of truth..."

Next, He takes the form of Faith and seduces Joseph, while Hope has a fruit and vegetable salad. Then it really gets disturbing when 'father' gets into the action. Of course, one can tell who The Devil takes the form of by the blue eyeliner each of the characters wear and Hope now seems fulfilled and liberated from sanctimonious guilt.

Distressed, Faith seeks solace with mother, who inspects her to see if her hymen is still intact. Supposedly, if her suspicions are correct, that Joseph seemed "possessed", if it was a demon, then she should still be intact. But when 'father' spots himself consorting with Hope, the illusion is shattered, and is attacked by hell hounds. After the inspection, turns out she is still a virgin; but then The Devil appears and transforms again for another rather disturbing scenario... then it's off to The Witch's Sabbath!

When Hope is whisked away in a puff of red smoke, father and Joseph team up, and armed with wooden crosses, scour the forest in search of it. Cut to extensive scenes of deviant merry-making, 'neath lunar, red and amber light, where almost every conceivable orgiastic perversion is enacted as described by paranoid superstition, including the infamous 'Besse Infame', and much, much more. At one point, a woman is multiply-mounted until they are what appears to be one copulating beast. Now, the so-called "sacrifice" is prepared, which is not an actual killing, but actually a symbolic term to signify the introduction of this maiden into the pleasures of the flesh. But before this, Joseph and father' find the spot, and rescuing Faith, are met with a defiant Hope exclaiming,

"Go 'F' yourself in Heaven! You have ruined it all with your c*cks of impurity! I'll cut your balls off! Especially Joseph's!...

When admonished to rebuke Satan, she further proclaims,

"Never! I'll eat My own sh*t before I renounce My Lord, and Master of all desire!" At which point she perishes when the cross is applied... or did she?

The ending scene features The Devil gazing up, as if talking to "God", observing that if he was as prompt at answering prayers as Ol' Nick was, then there would not be so much trouble; at which point he envelops Hope in his cape and escorts her to meet with the rest of the "flock".

Devil Inside Her seems to be a combination of Young Goodman Brown and The Blood on Satan's Claw, though overall, this piece of celluloid could very well be described as "shock porn".

Seduction of Amy

{X A.S. A.K.A., "Phantasmes". Written & Directed by Jean Rollin. Starring Jean-Pierre Bouyxou, Catherine Castel, Marie-Pierre Castel, Alban Ceray, Mylene D'Antes, Corinne Lemoine, Mannuella Marino, Greg Masters, Rachel Mhas, Marlène Myller, Jean Rollin, Stéphane Saratoga, Monica Swinn, Evelyne Thomas, Jean-Louis Vattier, Claudia Zante. 69 minutes.}

he film begins with some mutant attempting to rape a lovely girl, and ends up striking her who falls into a lake, and is rescued by an immortal man inhabiting a glorious mansion, who is also related to The Marquis DeSade. This presentation is seemingly based in large part upon The Count of Monte Cristo by Alexandre Dumas.

Strange sexual rites were performed in a lower chamber, resulting in his everlasting condition, which features carvings, statues, he explains as he leads her through the manse, where its other inhabitants take their pleasures with each other for great mutual gratification, and where "Amy" learns the pleasures of the flesh herself, despite some inner contention, which she sheds upon the realization of her own blossoming body and her growing love for this mysterious man.

This precious maiden he rescued at the marsh takes his heart, destined to be his companion at least for another many years, as he persists unto timelessness, preserving her sweet memory.

This sinemaerotica is remarkable for its beautiful natural and aristocratic environments, attractive performers {including two lovely twins, a gorgeous redhead, the sweetly erotic Amy, and an Indian beauty}, indulgent situations, elegant accoutrement {befitting nobility}, with a plot that is much more thought-out than usual, actually complimenting the overall production.

5/5

Devil's Due

{Produced by Nino DeRoma, directed by Ernest Danna}

"Worshipping The Devil... it's the 'in thing' to do!"

When "Cindy" is traumatized in her home town by what she perceives to be "evil men"*, from being slipped a mickey by the High School's Dean who has his way with her in his office {she was actually a valedictorian; but if she reported him, he would deny it claiming she incited it, then she would no longer be valedictorian}, her boyfriend refusing to marry her after she discovers she is pregnant, to her best friend "Barbie" bedding down with her father {whereupon walking in on them, screams and loses her voice from the shock}, deciding all men are animals who are only interested in using women

for sex. So she escapes to the big city seeking room mates and a new life, but who also just so happen to be members of a devil cult , inviting her to participate in their sex rites involving "Kampala", the supposed incarnation of The Devil.

"We believe that evil outweighs the good in the world, and as such, it is Satan who is our true savior."

Being that no one can view the rites of the cult except those initiated, she is lain naked upon The Altar, where Kampala appears in a white robe amidst bursts from a fog machine, who then begins screaming "the holy words" with His Chief Mistress 'Dawn':

"Satan is our savior!" At which point both begin enjoying her nubile body, and is "initiated".

After relating her troubled past to the other girls, they take compassion upon her which of course, yields to a lesbian scene. She considers Kampala to be a phony, only using the cult for the girls and for money. Now they reveal a secret of theirs to her - that they have been planning on taking over the cult for themselves. So at the very next ceremony, strichnine has been added to the ceremonial oil which is to be anointed upon the girl's breasts; so Kampala is challenged to prove his power, that all he has to do is just lay upon the Altar without partaking of the new succubus' breasts while she "rides the beast", as it were, but yields to temptation. Thus deceased, Cindy and Dawn are now the leaders of the cult. A lengthy celebratory orgy follows.

Now a "High Priestess", she decides to gain revenge against those who "fractured her life" as she put it, and calling each one, invites them for a visit...

3/5

---

* Interesting to note that this attitude primarily originated in the 60's & 70's, wherein much of the gender-based ad-hominem terminology developed as a result of a veneer of erstwhile 'strength' to mask reactionary weakness, instead of pro-actionary evolution.

Disc II

Sorceress

A young couple decide to hang out a shingle and go into the "psychic biz", with her as a palm reader and he as a secret photographer behind a two-way mirror, to frame rich clients out of money. This healthy couple are quite communicative, wherein she fulfills two fantasies for him - one of a Spanish Princess and another as a French maid.

She sets up by donning a black robe, displaying a red candle, and scenes to the tune of The Exorcist's "Tubular Bells"; if they only concentrate, each client's fantasies are fulfilled: One desires a dancer, another a young virgin, and another's desires are for another woman {Lesbian scene}. However, they were not counting on the mysterious man {probably a hired goon} who enters one day, rapes and strangles her, then places

her body into the convenient coffin propped up in the parlor with the Fiji mermaid dangling therefrom. Seems their chicanery was appreciated none too much by certain folks.

Interestingly, the boyfriend is no where to be found...

3/5

Suckula

{VIII A.S. Directed by Anthony Spinelli. Starring Pat Arno, Ann Finn, Art Gill. 54 minutes.}

In a comedic sex pulp men's magazine format, a-la in a very "Monty Python" style, the entire film is told from the position of a news reporter named "George Smutnam" in New York, relating the strange Vampiric happenings in Los Angeles, compiled by adventurous cameramen at great risk to themselves, chronologing alleged Vampire activity.

From the phallic cologne bottle commercial featuring masturbating model "Laura-Jean", to the efforts of Dracula / Suckula {the fanged actor actually has a necktie instead of the usual bow-tie} seducing several maidens, and indulging in both mutually-pleasurable oral and blood fetishes {particularly a very talented young lady with a perfectly-placed Devil's Mark}; an amusing Folger's coffee commercial featuring a couple sharing their intimate relations; to "Sandra VanOcre" {a hilariously mustached man in drag} for an abrupt interview with "Rodney Alucard the IIIrd", a direct descendant of Count Dracula. Then on to a parody of those "Go see Cal" Worthington car ads, complete with modified lyrics and a negro slave girl; then back to Sandra for an interview with a female vampire named "Moona Lisa" who virtually cannibalizes her/him; now please view your monitor for another seemingly gratuitous scene of a couple having sex, when the girl surprisingly turns into a vampire; then a final exchange with Sandra who meets a predictably temporary demise by the fangs of Alucard and Moona.

"Remember... you were there! ...And now for the late movie, 'The Mad Motorcycle Monster Who Ate Naked Hippies'. Thank you, and Good Night."

5/5.

The Last Step Down

{V A.S. A.K.A., "Even Devils Pray". Written by Arthur Allen, Phil Miller. Directed by Lawrence Ramport. Starring Uschi Digard, Olivia James, Terri Johnson, Malta, Beatrice Stolen, Michael Valentine. 67 minutes.}

The remarkably Satantric opening scene displays robed figures filing in to a church containing an ankh-like insignia on the wall, where the Phallus is risen forth to the congregants as if a "monstrance", dipping it into a chalice, and anointing its contents upon two female initiates, who writhe in carnal ecstasy, are brought to orgasm, whom are thoroughly and passionately enjoyed

After seducing a nubile acolyte, these Satantric "Nuns" bring her forth into the Chambers of Lust where during this veritable Satantric Mass, is initiated into the pleasures of the flesh, collectively enjoyed by the congregants upon The Altar, until all find release.

During a discussion between the girls, they affirm the benefits of these healthy and naturally indulgent psychodramatic practices, with the neophyte stating that she had no idea that there were so many positions... Herein there are no sacrifices, no gore, no death or misery, just the life-affirming delights of the earth, promoting overall success, strength of character and ego. A great viewing pleasure.

5/5

Bonus Shorts

Witch Sabbath {Hexen Sabbat}: This one is essentially a music video, to the tunes of what sounds like Siouxie & The Banshees and David Bowie, in dim flickering candle light with robed and disrobed participants having group sex, who are apparently initiating a cute young woman into their Gothic-like cult, somewhat reminiscent of The Khlysty - there is even one participant who resembles Rasputin included. It is later revealed that one of the seemingly male participants is actually a girl wearing a strap-on, who joins in the fun with both the initiate and the others. Silver crosses abound.

Satanist: A diabolical man resembling Tim Skerrit, hypnotizes a voluptuous girl resembling a mannequin, using his fascination pendant, to perform his every desire, and she does... to his great satisfaction.

Lucifer's Lust {A.K.A., "'F' For Peace"}: A robed and bearded Lucifer appears to a couple, directing them to perform various "unspeakable" pleasurable acts, working them like puppets to sin well for his viewing pleasure. They are to remember in their dreams what Lucifer has taught them, for their carnal benefit. Here The Devil represents a sense of adventure and sexploration, instructing this previously boring couple to improve their sex lives, and they are all the better for it.

Disc III

Satan's Sex Slaves

Satan appears as a black-robed man roaming a carnival in white and red split face makeup, visiting several lustfully-unfortunate persons with promises of carnal indulgence, if they only give their 'souls' to Him, each of which becomes fulfilled. From the lonesome Victorian "Lady Violet DeGamba" who happily beds down with a blacksmith; to an impotent man healed of his malady, that he may be able to consummate his marriage, becomes generously endowed, receiving two succubi for his pleasure; and a frustrated, curious girl who desires satisfaction, experiences her every desire.

This film seems to assert that The Devil is a friend to man, despite the rottenly sanctimonious ingratitude expressed by the couple in the end, claiming that the restored virility allowed them to consummate their love by marriage, yet were only wed because of His bestowance, and so He is cheated from his rightful due. So it is supposed that as long as they indulge with only each other for the rest of their lives {thus avoiding "adultery"}, their souls are 'safe'. He departs with diabolic laughter, knowing full well he will claim his due in time.

4/5

Blue Voodoo

When a pretty young stripper is treated shamefully by her scumbag boyfriend {particularly rotten considering he stole money she gathered by all means necessary for their marriage, only to decide at the last moment - right after fellatio, in fact - that he had not intend to marry her at all}, a beautiful Witch comes to her aid after she becomes aware of the incident by viewing her on the Magic Mirror in her fog-permeated Chamber.

Depressed, the girl wishes for death. Seems he suddenly became infatuated by another young stripper with a really impressive act. The Witch calls upon "The Black Widow" by the power of Damballa to rightfully punish the lowlife.

After The Witch and The Black Widow enjoy each other, they conveniently become employed in the very same club, where The Black Widow teaches three guidos some culture by transporting them to Nero's Rome, resulting in quite a delightful spectacle of orgiastic indulgence. The Black Widow weaves her spell upon the audience, and eventually gains the attention of the boyfriend, whose life force is absorbed in a very intriguing way.

This film is primarily enjoyable for the "Black Magic" displayed, the succulent 'witches', the creatively-entertaining dance performances, and the Bacchanalian spectacle.

4/5.

Sexorcist Devil

{IX A.S. A.K.A., "Undressed To Kill", "The Sexorcist", The Sexorcist's Devil". Directed by Ray Dennis Steckler. Written by Arnold Blatt. Starring Lilly Lamarr, Kelly Guthrie, Eva Gaulant, Wayne Williams. 61 minutes.}

"There is a beast in man that should be "{s}exercised, not exorcised." ASLV / DB.

Done in a documentary style, Carolyn is a reporter researching an article for an Occult magazine, and decides to accompany "occult expert & Sexorcist*" Dr. Von Kleinsmidt to "The Marsh" {a blighted (super) natural wilderness akin to The Devil's Canyon}, a dangerous environment steeped in nefarious superstition about a "sex-crazed Devil worship cult" supposedly performing

rites of darkness out there, until he comes upon a mysterious box containing parchments, which he takes back with him to his study for translation. Unbeknownst to him, while he does so, he unwittingly calls forth a "perverse disciple of The Devil" named "Volta" {Wayne Williams} who takes possession of Diane's friend Janice, a prostitute he uses to seduce and kill everyone around her while taking his pleasures as well. He initiates her by bestowing a pendant displaying "Set" upon her, while together uttering "Hail Satan!" with uplifted Cornus.

When Carolyn becomes suspicious after a phone call to Diane, she returns home to find her afflicted with a demon trying to possess her, but it is all a ruse, and surprisingly, she is also dispatched, as is her pimp, but not before Von Kleinsmidt is alerted, who attempts to battle these "evil spirits" by using passages from The Goetia {The 'Lesser Key of Solomon', a blindlight tome by a blindlight author, who was subservient to the mythological Jehovic god}, admonishing demons to submit, yet because of Volta's quick efforts {with a gesture used by Crowley to signify horns on the sides of the head}, manages to materialize a knife in the hand of the possessed Diane, who stabs Von Kleinsmidt to death. A smiling Volta proclaims success, that Satan's will has been fulfilled, and walks back into the wilderness...

Mentionable are some of the intriguing paintings in Von Kleinsmidt's office {Satan arising, embracing a witch; a Reaper goosing a Lilithian witch holding a serpent, perhaps representing the kundalini; a demonic beast tearing prey limb from limb; and a portrait of the setting sun in The West}, which do resemble Dr. LaVey's style, and the recurrent appearance of an image of a lion resembling Togare. Also, the appearance of a Baphomet in the ending credits.

3/5

---

* According to the film, "Sexorcism" is "removing The Devil from your body while he's sexually possessing it."

Disc IV

Hotter Than Hell
VI A.S.

Beginning with a delightfully lustful scene in Hell, Satan is enthroned wielding a sword receives a curious message that not as many souls are being damned, so he orders His two sons to ascend to earth to find out why this is so. While one is more committed to the duty, the other is rather comedically Lokian in countenance {rather like Little Nicky}, making for several humorous commentaries and situations. They seek to "corrupt" as many maidens as they can, but it seems that time and time again they are met with salacious women where the question of who is seducing who is contemplated.

Manifesting in demonic attire, they appear to a couple of salacious female room mates, concluding in a foursome; a stoner girl, a succulent virgin {wherein she is seduced after consuming a bubbling elixir made by 'dad'}, and a desperate brunette secretary, moving from an office desk to a rocking horse, where among other pleasing acts, perform "arabian style" [seated intercourse}.

Upon descending back to Hell to report with the secretary who subsequently expresses her wish to be a part of the plan to "corrupt all mankind", their passion unabated, continue their activities under the approving and enthusiastic gaze of Satan, wherein He also takes His pleasure after uttering the "Invocation Employed for The Conjuration of Lust" from The Satanic Bible!

With more effort placed into this production, this film stands out primarily for the choice of music {more than just the usual jazz, with some Middle-Eastern, some instrumental, and some tribal drumming thrown into the cauldron}; more attention paid to props & costumes {The Devil appearing quite Bacchus / Pan-like, in a fur suit, upon a throne, with sword, and the devilish attire of the sons}; the decent acting & personalities {the Lokian son is quite funny at times, and it seems the fatherly-endearing actor playing Satan actually has acting experience}; casting {well placed and hypothetically believable}, lighting {with uses of red, green and fire light}, sets {cave-like environment with hell fire and boulders, one of which is termed "The Altar"}; credits {several humorous animations of a horny seducing devil}, and the amusingly comedic plot, all make for an exceptional sinemaerotic gem overall.

5/5

Night of The Warlock

Amusingly, on a hand-written title and a typed paper printout, this film claims to be a comprehensive display of authentic occult rites, as well as all six "principals" of 'Satanic Films, Inc.' met with violent death by fire, as an entertaining tie-in with the plot. Also obvious propaganda employed for entertainment purposes, much like the warning on the Necronomicon book.

The film begins in a darkly draped chamber with a young lady strapped to a black platform who is "violated" by a young and pretty black lingerie-wearing 'witch' wearing a hip harness with a prosthetic phallus, while being observed by two cult members in robes. The Altar features a crudely-drawn red star upon which is super-imposed a vague white geometrical goat head, black candles, and a skull. Unfortunately, the young lady meets with a grisly demise.

Her sister seeks to discover what happened to her because of the suspicious death, though unbeknownst to her, she employs the very men who are responsible for her immolation. Her boyfriend is payed a visit from the incognito witch, hypnotizing him via her seductive wiles, while the sister is also hypnotized by the head cultist's scorpion pendant, where she is made to disrobe and is taken sexually on the office table.

Because she perceives their actions are unjustified, the young witch is punished via a whipping because of her disobedience to the cult. While copulating upon the platform in the ritual chamber, the boyfriend is "violated" by the harness, followed by she being punished again, when all that is left of her is a skeleton with a strap-on.

The sister is kidnapped and taken to the chamber where she is raped by the cultists, and just as she is also to meet with the same fate as her sister, police sirens send them on their way, but also meet with a fiery demise themselves during the escape. The film concludes with a Rosemary's Baby inference, and thus, The Devil prevails again.

Throughout the movie, a demonic face appears from time to time, as if to assert the presence of The Devil. Where this production lacks in funds and effects, it makes up in imagination.

2/5.

Madam Satan

A psychic-buster seeks to expose the psychic biz, arranging an appointment under the pretense of attending a séance conducted by a 'Madam Cobra'; the three attending couples are Magically transported into the dark recesses of a sex cult where they participate in sex rites, and their fetishes are indulged.

Madam Cobra is actually Madam Satan, a Dominatrix who appears in black lingerie, boots with stiletto heels, and a cape, while others disrobe. They are led nude down a hallway to the sounds of a storm and herded by a man with a whip into a chamber where a caped "priest" awaits, reading from "his" bible, which are actually segments from The Seventh Enochian Key from The Satanic Bible.

The group imbibe an "elixir of love", and begin indulging in the delights of the flesh, except for one member who does not seem too responsive, so it is up to Madam Satan to figure out what his particular fetish is; so after a whipping, and with the aid of an inserted vibrator, he finds release. All the while observing the festivities, the priest signifies the Cornu, preserving all in attendance with the perspective of indulging in The Devil's pleasures.

When all are satisfied, they are materialized and returned to the "séance table" with no one the wiser. As to the investigator, it seems it was he who was exposed in the end!

This is actually a great fictional premise, and would like to see this film remade in higher quality.

3/5.

Emerson NR303TT Heritage Series 4-in-1 Home Music System

I was pleased to receive the "Emerson NR303TT Heritage Series 4-in-1 Home Music System" recently, which now compliments The Noctuary splendidly. The antique smooth wooden finish design with all the modern features as well, being both aesthetically and technologically pleasing is a wonderful combination. It almost seems like these retro-innovations were made with the discerning Satanist in mind. In today's disposable society, where in many cases the herd's "past" is our present, from rare collectibles, to scouring antique shops for rare treasures, furniture, and objects d'art, this combines the best of both worlds in one.

Record turntable

I do have a penchant to collect rare vinyl, for the artistic, evocative, and arcane sonic value. Considering I also have preserved much of My first purchases from Draclinghood, this will be quite interesting, much better than the rather bland current models. Plus, the liftable top also provides for a nice pedistal for a bust or statuette.

Cassette Player

Located on the side, with which to listen to My extensive collection of tapes, some of which have been incrementally collected on CD as well, but much of which are both irreplaceable and contain sentimental value as well.

AM/FM features

Tuning knobs with spindle pointing to station numbers, the yellowish light, provide for a particularly evocative experience, even with that certain whistling sound while changing between stations. At times, it almost seems as if one is receiving stations from the golden era of radio.

CD player

The black planchette is contained behind a decorative silver finish design and is completely unobtrusive for one's total environment theme.

There is no denying the time travel dynamic which occurs when using this entertainment system, as well as others in the line, wherein one feels as if transported and preserved into the misty corridors of one's timeless preference. These types of 'retro-designs' have been available for a few years now, and in My opinion, it behooves the Satanist interested in cultural anthropology to take advantage of their recreation.

House of Netherworld

Anton LaVey Pendent

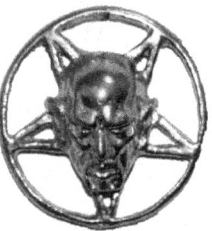

The Anton Szandor LaVey pentagram pendant is a pleasing tribute to the iconically-immortal founder of The Church of Satan. Thick and heavy silver finish measuring in at 1 1/4" in diameter, with wonderful detail, it is truly a great addition to the Satanist's collection.

Anton LaVey Bust

The Anton LaVey bust is a tribute to the founder of the Church of Satan, an amazing and brilliant writer , musician, magician and a great influence on all of here at the House of Netherworld. It has been sculpted in the Neo-Classical style of the late 19th century and reflects a refined and artistic sensibility. This will become the center piece of many an altar in the finest of lairs. Each bust is hand cast and hand finished in a Faux Bronze designer poly-resin and will outlast us all, an heirloom piece to be handed down through the ages. The Anton LaVey tribute bust stands over 11 inches tall and commands a sense of awe in all who see it. Embedded in the front piece of the bust is a reproduction of Dr LaVey's personal symbol, the lightening struck pentagram, cast in fine pewter and electroplated in sterling silver.

With special thanks to Witch Sara Rung proprietress of Femaledictions we are including a special blend granular incense called "Maestro" each bust will come with a tube filled with a generous portion of this special inaugural blend to sanctify your lair and welcome the Anton LaVey bust into your home.

The cost of this profound artwork is $135.00 + $15.00 shipping

These are produced and sent out on a first come-first served basis and shipping starts after April 11th 2008. Please act now to secure your piece of Satanic history before it is too late and this piece is sold out. You will not find another like it in this world or any other.

Netherworld Baphomet

With the crowning black flame blazing atop Baphomet's head, complete with the beard of wisdom and a gaze enlivened by the energy of the wearer, I have had the pleasure of possessing this remarkable item for some time, and again, with splendid attention paid to design, it assuredly adds quite an ambiance to The Ritual Chamber and/or one's ritualistic accoutrement, when so inclined. Highly recommended for that striking statement.

h o u s e o f n e t h e r w o r l d . c o m

Satanic Serenades
~ Black Heart Poetry ~

All Is Well In Hell
March 31, XLIII

Cats yowling and hissing
by Satan's Hollow
Hell hounds howl into
the night
Spiders upon the walls with
their prey
The music of wind chimes
softly play...

The scent of black earth and
jasmine float in the air
As the orchestra sounds through
arcane angles
Such pleasing perfection
Halloween is here and will
never leave
In this haunted house of
nocturnal dreams...

Embraced in darkness by the
amber lamp
With the flicker of Tesla's
nucleus
Glowing in the somber chamber
Phantom visions surrounding
All is well in Hell...

Fete Diaboli

Candlelight
A glass of wine
Reflecting crimson sight
Bacchus' kiss upon the lips
Imbibe the Devil's sip...

A feast presented
Black Grace splendid
Velvet darkness
Time suspended
Embracing blushing skin...

To the sound of rain pervading
The gentle breeze of whispered flailing...

Oracles of apparition
Ignites the dancing muse
Sweet Nocturnal celebration
A toast to life of sin unending
Sealed with wax milieu...

Black Dragon Phoenix
2/1/XLIII

The Wheel has turned, by
season's churn
Blackest flames twist and
burn
Infernal Dragon birthed
The sphere is one, the sphere is
none
A timeless secret not undone...

Passing through the looking glass
Travel through the chasm vast
Reflection manifest The Will
Emerge in the eternal now...

Rejuvenation, transformation
The fires within purify
Crossing through the swirling gate
The Third Eye opens wide...

In the darkness of regeneration
The serpent sheds its skin
Omnipotent visualization
Begins anew again...

Drawing deep, the shadow fang
Piercing eyes, and heart, and brain
Immortal form, Hellish born...

Black Phoenix flies, forever night!
In Power, Joy, unending Might!

Why Old Men Smile
by Tier Instinct

A knock at my door
like thunder above
no one can find her
she's gone...my love,

How did they know
they have come so fast
the deed just done
so fresh in the past,

Still she waits there
on the bathroom floor
they will not notice
so I take to the door,

Cookies for sale
yes scouts never lie
dark blessings from hell
I had found my alibi,

I dumped her downtown
naked and bruised
she had been raped
so it said on the news,

Men in blue they came alright
innocent they said
he had not
killed his wife,

The money from the insurance
has made me rich
I sometimes start to cry
thinking about that bitch!

Your Journey is about to begin. Enter At Your Own Risk!

A Poetic Horror Adventure into the
realms of Urban legend and madness!

reocities.com/dblackthorne/DevilsCanyon/
DC_entrance

Loki's Laughter

Devilutions: Comparisons between Draconis Blackthorne & the Damien Thorn character

Damien Thorn was created as a proposed characterization of what "The Antichrist" may be like throughout formation. Realizing that a Satanist places no serious stock in christian superstition, this is merely an amusing comparison of some of the eerie similarities between the character of Damien Thorn and the actual person of Draconis Blackthorne, which occurs to us whenever we watch The Omen series:

Draconis Blackthorne born in U.S.A., spent preschool years in Italy. Subsequently went to official "Vatican school" until relocating to the U.S. to attend private school. Also attended various Martial Arts schools. Damien Thorn born in Italy, spent infancy there until moving to U.S.A., where he attended military school.

DB baptized at The Vatican, kept snuffing candle, spit on floor. Upon self-realization as a Satanist, later used baptismal candle in Satanic Baptism ceremony, which went up like a torch. DT writhed when approaching church.

DB had a doberman, bull mastiff, and a German shepherd as guardian and companion. DT had a doberman as guardian and companion.

DB has a so-called "remolino" {Italian and Spanish for 'whirlpool', or 'tornado'} hair configuration at back of scalp. Noted and remarked by parents. Also has an interesting 'hakenkruz' {which in certain Occult circles represents 'the black sun' / "Sorath" = 666, 'numerologically'} 'grammadon' configuration upon anatomy. DT has so-called "mark of the beast" swirling birthmark on scalp.

Dark Forces activate when either are threatened, punishing those who deserve it, and otherwise brings fortune to those who benefit them.

DB has an uncanny affinity with certain predatory animals, such as large dogs, cats, rats, monkeys, snakes and spiders. DT has a mental connection with that doberman in the film, while most other animals are apparently frightened of him.

DB as a Dracling also a child with dark hair and eyes, pale skin, with similar build {to the original}.

Both entrepreneurs went on to found businesses.

Both were born on interesting dates: DB at 6:03 {6+0+3=9} on February 1st, "Candlemas Eve" {thus conceived on Walpurgisnacht}; DT at 6:06, June 6th, ergo, '666'.

As a side note, DB's Mother had a dream of a demon by a raging river {"Styx"? "Acheron"? "Phlegethon"?; see Dante's Inferno} while pregnant. A bent tree in the shape of a crucifix tumbled into the water. The Rosemary Woodhouse character in Rosemary's Baby dreamt of copulation with The Devil.

Overall, is there 'something' to it? Maybe so, maybe not, you decide...

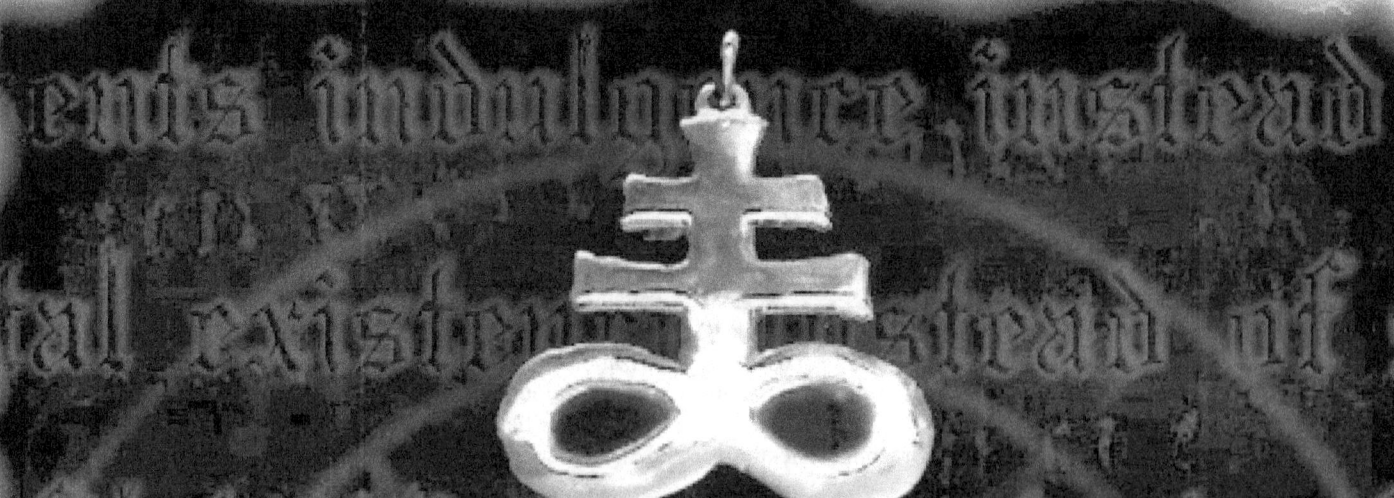

Now Available from
~The Church of Satan Emporium~
Brimstone pendant by Magister Robert A. Lang

This is the Alchemy symbol for Brimstone / Sulfur made popular as a Satanic symbol because of its use in the Satanic Bible by Anton Szandor LaVey as the seal placed above the 9 Satanic statements. Symbolically it can also be related to the tree of life with the figure eight (the twisted Ouroborous forever swallowing its tail or Leviathan) symbolizing infinity and the eternal motion of creation evolution and destruction and as well the strong deep roots of the Ygdrassil tree. The 5 branches symbolize the 5 senses of course (seeing, hearing, touching, tasting, smelling) with the center shaft representing the trunk of the tree or if you will the human spine connecting all. In essence one must know where one comes from and must have firm roots planted deep in earthy darkness before one 'should' sprout the branches ascending to what is undefiled wisdom. Without strong roots there can be no lasting branches for when they reach too high the foundation collapses and the tree dies.

Here is a limited edition beautiful version of that symbol hand crafted and sculpted in wax then cast in Sterling Silver by artist Robert A. Lang.

Weight: 12 grams
Height: 1 3/4 inches
Width: 1 1/4 inches

COSEMPORIUM.COM

ASATRU

By Kyle Whittaker

I know what you are thinking. What was I thinking? Writing something about Asatru in a Satanic publication? Yep, that is what I have done. Why? The simple answer is that it was something personal. I have always known that I was of European descent, but wasn't sure what to make of it. I wanted to connect to that, so I went searching, and my quest led me to study Asatru.

What is Asatru?

Asatru is the modern version of the pre-Christian religion of the ancient Germanic people. It essentially is a native religion, much like the religion of the Native American Indians. It is a tribal religion that honors ancestry, and shows how we are connected to the natural world. Asatru is a polytheistic religion that honors the Gods and Goddesses of the pre-Christian Germanic people. In Asatru the names of the Norse Gods and Goddesses are used, primarily because there is more information available on them. At first I wasn't sure about studying Asatru mainly because of it being a spiritual religion, but the more I researched, the more I saw that it has nothing to do with anything supernatural. I am not going to go headlong in any details in the practices of Asatru. There are various websites one could look to.

A Personal Thought

Personally, I do find some value in the Asatru religion. As a Satanist, I do question the need for there to be any spirituality associated with it. If mainly for ritual and ceremony, that's fine. So far I do not see a slave mentality to it. There is an emphasis on community, but there is respect for personal individuality. Although there is a belief in an afterlife, it is not a main focal point. Much like Satanism, Asatru advocates living in the here and now. What Asatru considers virtues are as follows: strength, courage, joy, honor, freedom, loyalty to kin, realism, vigor, and the revering of our ancestors. From my point of view I find many of these to be compatible with Satanism. The vices in Asatru that are to be avoided are as follows: weakness, cowardice, adherence to dogma rather than to the realities of the world, and the like. Aside from the spirituality aspect, I feel that taking parts of the Asatru religion and incorporating them in my daily rituals could be productive. I am my own God, and can use whatever means to externalize that. In closing, I'd like to say that it is wise to honor one's ancestry. One must know his/her history in order to understand who they are now. For me Asatru has given me a way to connect with my ancestry. The main point is be proud of who you are no matter how unpopular it may be. For more information on the Asatru visit the links at the bottom. For those who are not of Germanic descent, look to your own culture's mythology, and values. They are a part of the self.

http://www.runestone.org or http://www.asatru.org

Spadra Cemetery
{A.K.A., "Old Settler's Cemetery", Pomona, CA}

Located near train tracks and a freeway, and set about 200 feet from the road, relatively hidden from view, that the casual passer-by would miss this intriguing location, is Spadra Cemetery, an odd little bone yard dating back to the 1800's, complete with a rust-worn decrepit sign. Having an abandoned look to it, a couple of tombstones are actually toppled over.

Myself and a couple of acquaintances had entered this rather intimate cemetery one crisp autumn evening for a perusal into this legendary graveyard. As tends to be the case, an eerie silence graces this memorial park, spanning only about a couple of blocks in diameter, yet when one enters, one receives the impression of a vast, desolate, and windswept environment, reminiscent of an Old Western horror movie.

There is a pleasant grove of willow trees shielding the place from freeway view, semi-circling from within. It is from here that the supposed sounds of phantom footsteps and crashing have emminated This over-looming spot may very well be a salacious location for carnal indulgence as well.

I have long-since heard of various haunted activity occurring here, from the shadow of a man believed to be that of 'James Fryer' seen sometimes disappearing into his tombstone, and if visitors become unruly, a sensation of being stabbed, pushed, or strangled, is claimed to have been felt by those who misbehave.

A mysterious hot wind manifests, followed by sensations of tugging at clothing and the laughter of ghostly children "Bertie & Ernest", to being tripped. Objects dematerialize from one location, only to reappear in another one nearby which had not yet been visited, as if leading the observer to take a tour. Humorously, I have heard of someone leaving their beverage on a tombstone, only to have it reappear on another plot at the other end of the property.

The Blake Family graves yield a nurturing maternal woman protectively embracing young women who near there, accompanied by the scent of floral perfume.

The cemetery has since sadly been closed for renovation due to vandalism, and is cared for the Pomona Renovation Society, to be re-opened when proper measures have been attended to. The nearby Blake Mansion has recently been opened for tours, which had for a long time been considered haunted as well {with a splendid view of Spadra Cemetery}, and now provides the interested with the veritable {educational} ghosts of history.

The Devil's Web

Church of Satan
[Churchofsatan.com]
Welcome to The Infernal Empire

Shadowmantium
[Shadowmantium.cjb.net]
Official Website of Warlock Draconis Blackthorne

Anton Szandor LaVey Archives
[Geocities.com/DBlackthorne/LaVeyArchives.html]
Bibliographic arcana from the collection of Draconis Blackthorne.

FANGORIA Musick Blog
[Fangoria.com/blogs]
Reviews by Zoth Ommog & Draconis Blackthorne.

Artistic Devil
[Artisticdevil.com]
An iconoclastic and diabolical artistry resource

Old Nick
[oldnick.com]
A publication of Satanically-Salacious tricks and treats.

Satannet
[satannet.com]
Letters to The Devil, Undercroft, CoS Emporium

Inside The Church of Satan
[insidethechurchofsatan.com]
Church of Satan documentary by Joshua P. Warren

Black House Tribute CD
[Blackhousetribute.com]

Purging Talon Publishing
[purgingtalon.com]
Purging Talon multimedia, Not Like Most Magazine, The Sinister Screen.

Asylum of Satan
[Asylumofsatan.com]
Magister Rex Diabolos Church's Gallery of Aesthetic Terrorism

Radio Free Satan
[Radiofreesatan.com]
Eclectic radio by Citizens of The Infernal Empire

The Quintessentials
[thequintessentials.com]
Satanic Punk for The Elite!

Coffin Rust
[CoffinRust.com]
The darksome artisty of Warlock Daniel Byrd.

Headless Historicals
[Headlesshistoricals.com]
Headless dolls of the executed. Favored by Wednesday Addams.

Superhighway to Hell
[purgingtalon.com/sth]
"The definitive guide to Satanism online"

Bolt of The Goat
[Boltofthegoat.com]
Dark Somewhere magazine, The Art of Michael K. Silva

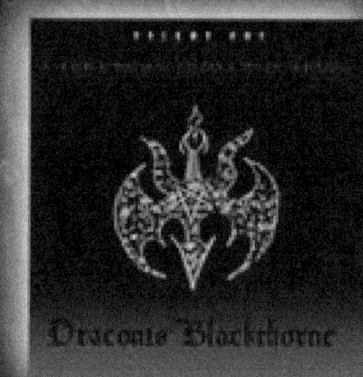

Shadow Gallery Calendar
XLV A.S.

stores.lulu.com/DBlackthorne